Ghosts and the Japanese

The ghost of a bamboo flute (hitoyogiri, *a kind of* shakuhachi) *appears between the waves. Artist and date unknown.*

Ghosts and the Japanese

Cultural Experience in Japanese Death Legends

by Michiko Iwasaka
and Barre Toelken

Utah State University Press
Logan, Utah
1994

Utah State University Press
Logan, Utah 84322-7800

This publication was supported in part by the College of Humanities, Arts, and Social Sciences, Utah State University.

Cover painting by Setsuō, reproduced, by permission, from the original in the Zenshōan Temple, Tokyo.

Cover and book design by Scott Engen.

Typeset in TEX from WordPerfect files by The Bartlett Press, Inc.

Library of Congress Cataloging-in-Publication Data

Iwasaka, Michiko, 1945-
    Ghosts and the Japanese : cultural experience in Japanese death legends / by Michiko Iwasaka and Barre Toelken
       p. cm.
    Includes bibliographical references (p.   ) and index.
    ISBN 0-87421-179-4
    1. Folklore—Japan. 2. Death—Japan—Folklore. 3. Death—Social aspects—Japan. 4. Legends—Japan—History and criticism. 5. Funeral rites and ceremonies—Japan. 6. Japan—Social life and customs. I. Toelken, Barre. II. Title.
GR340.I868   1994
398.2'0952'05—dc20   94-17577
                                              CIP

Respectfully dedicated to Kunio
Iwasaka

The ghosts of a married couple carrying a skull. Artist: Ōtai (other information unknown).

Contents

Illustrations

Color plates in Part III

Hototogisu, the ghost of a prostitute in a Kabuki play

Utagawa Shigesumi at the Otaki waterfall

Kohada Koheiji, the murdered husband in a Kabuki play

A woman's ghost holding a severed head

David J. Hufford

Foreword

Ghosts and the Japanese is a fine book that has both great scholarly merit and broad appeal. In it Michiko Iwasaka and Barre Toelken describe Japanese death customs, provide translations of contemporary Japanese ghost legends, and place both within their cultural and historical context. In the process Iwasaka and Toelken have illustrated the many ways in which such legends not only reflect deep cultural values but also are a central part of the dynamic process by which those values are shaped, maintained, and transmitted. This thorough cultural account is greatly enriched by illustrations drawn from rare Japanese art work portraying ghosts. The book does a remarkable job of addressing three important and fascinating topics.

Because of the careful attention to the cultural context of these stories, this book will be of great interest to all who study narratives and cultural process. It also provides an excellent introduction to Japanese culture at a time when growing political and economic ties have greatly increased the need for Westerners to understand Japan. No amount of history or economic theory can provide the human understanding that comes with the kind of encounter with values, beliefs, and world-view that Iwasaka and Toelken have provided. The result is an introduction to central ideas that underlie everyday life in Japan, a crucial domain too often overlooked in typical efforts to "sum up" a culture. And yet it is precisely this domain that is necessary for graceful and comfortable interaction, as Iwasaka and Toelken clearly illustrate in their "Introduction to the Left Stairway."

Perhaps the broadest appeal of this book, though, lies in the way that it helps us to understand belief in ghosts, a concept found in all cultures and at all times of which we have any record. In their commentary on this ample set of well-translated narratives, the authors have clearly shown their distinctively Japanese quality and their relationship to traditional Japanese culture. At the same time, they have elucidated a great variety of ways in which individual stories, and the Japanese ghost tradition in general, parallel beliefs found in other cultures.

Their great success in high technology clearly shows the Japanese to be a "modern" people or, as it is often put in ethnocentric terms, "westernized." But as Iwasaka and Toelken point out, the changes in Japanese culture during the past several decades are very much like those that have occurred in the United States and Europe. It has often been assumed that this process of change destroys cultural continuity, and both Japanese and American society seem characterized by novelty and an apparently chaotic and fragmented eclecticism. Assumptions about modern discontinuity and fragmentation are strongest with regard to spiritual values. In Japan, Shinto, Buddhism, Confucianism, and Christianity mix in the practices of individuals and families, while a spate of new religions have sprung up since World War II. And, the authors point out, a great many Japanese, perhaps most, "belong" to no religion at all. Superficially this looks like a degradation of spirituality. And yet the stories in this book clearly show, as will a conversation with the average Japanese individual, that spiritual beliefs and values remain extremely strong and deep. This is the first of several direct parallels to the culture of the United States. Through much of this century sociologists believed Americans were becoming much less religious, only to discover late in the century that they had mistaken institutional religious affiliation for spirituality. The religious pluralism of the modern world creates a new and historically unique situation for the believer, what Peter Berger has called "the heretical impera-tive." A stolid attachment to a monolithic set of institutional forms becomes much more difficult when one is constantly faced with the beliefs and disbeliefs of many other traditions. In Japan and the United States this has led to a more eclectic approach, sometimes disparagingly called "cafeteria style religion," and to the rapid development of new and rapidly changing religious forms. The new religions of Japan, de-spite their clear cultural stamp, have a great deal in common with "New Age" spirituality in the West.

However upsetting modern religious changes are to the traditionalist, one thing is clear: they do not represent a de-cline in either spiritual belief or values. Neither do they represent a sharp break with historical traditions. Again, both in Japan and the United States these changes embody both cross-cultural assimilation and a persistence of an-cient beliefs. The assimilation is clearly a two-way street. Buddhist spiritual ideas such as *karma*, coming from Japan and other Asian cultures, have had an enormous impact on American spiritual ideas.

Perhaps more surprising is the discovery that the histori-cal continuities of belief, those that reach back to times before constant intercultural influences became the religious norm, also show a core of remarkable cross-cultural parallels. To some extent this reflects universals of ordinary human expe-rience. For example, a mother's desire to protect her children is common to all cultures, and many stories all over the world involve the intervention of a mother's ghost on behalf of her child. Iwasaka and Toelken have provided numerous ex-amples of such stories. In Japan these stories of parent child connection often have a very Confucian appearance, sup-porting filial piety. Others reflect earlier Japanese concepts about the dangers of unritualized babies. These influences give the narratives a distinctive cultural stamp. Such sto-ries found in North America have many differences, but one does not need a strong tradition of ancestor veneration to understand the idea of maternal love that can reach beyond the grave. The importance of culturally distinct features should not be allowed to obscure the common humanity displayed in cultural traditions as the authors show in their trenchant criticism of Joseph Campbell's characterization of Asian religions as treating individuals as unimportant.

Perhaps more startling than the recognizable recurrence of ordinary human experience in ghost narratives is the appearance of parallels in the details of distinctly *non-ordinary* experience. For example, the story of the audible death omens that Iwasaka and Toelken recount is essentially identical to narratives that I have encountered in Canada and the United States—right down to the details of hearing the sound of hammering nails into a coffin a number of days before the event. Many elements of the ghost ship and ghostly, drowned sailor stories are similarly striking in their parallels to narratives common on both sides of the North Atlantic.

I was particularly interested to find that vengeful child ghosts (*zashiki warashi*) are said sometimes to climb on and press the chest of a sleeping person, a readily recognizable feature of a set of beliefs about supernatural assault that I have documented in other parts of the world and associated with the medical phenomenon of sleep paralysis (1982). I have found other traditions in which this experience is explained by reference to a vengeful child. For example, I interviewed a man from Honduras who had been taught that the experience is caused by the attack of the spirit of an unbaptized infant. I have subsequently found the same event in the Japanese tradition of *kanashibari*, which may be translated as "to immobilize as if bound with metal chains." According to a recent Buddhist dictionary, *kanashibari* "is one of the spells of esoteric Buddhism to make one's opponent or a criminal immobile by the power of *Fudomyoo*, a Buddhist god" (Nakamura et al. 1989). *Kanashibari* is very well known in current Japanese tradition and is frequently depicted in the popular Japanese *manga* (comic books). Not only do the descriptions in these popular accounts make it clear that they refer to sleep paralysis, but the Japanese sleep literature has used *kanashibari* as the common term for the phenomenon (Fukuda 1987, 1989). This magical binding is similar to the meaning of the English term *spell bind*, and in many Western traditions it is also believed to be something that can be done through esoteric knowledge. It was a common accusation made against witches. This case illustrates very well the operation of a common core of experience embedded within distinctive local cultural forms. The ghostly *zashiki warashi* are not Buddhist adepts, and the two kinds of accounts have many different meanings. Here we can see a particular kind of non-ordinary experience receiving multiple interpretations within Japanese culture. And yet both Japanese interpretations of this terrifying paralysis can be found accompanying the same experience in other cultures.

The Japanese accounts presented by Iwasaka and Toelken are rich in experiential detail and make the identification of underlying experiences easier than is usually the case in folktale texts. This may be in part a reflection of the influence of Yanagita Kunio (1875–1962, whom Iwasaka and Toelken describe as the greatest single force in developing the study of *minzokugaku* (roughly, folklore). This remarkable person emphasized the importance of the subjective long before the current trends in "reflexive" scholarship. Having been pointed in the direction of Yanagita's work by Iwasaka and Toelken's account, I have found still more illustrations of cross-cultural experiential parallels. For example, in a recent translation of Yanagita's *The Legends of Tōno*, originally published in 1910, I found the following account:

THE TEMPLE GATE

Matsunojo Kikuchi of Iide was ill with an acute fever from exposure to the cold and would often lose his breath. He went out into the rice fields, and hurried off to the family temple of Kisei-in. When he would put a little effort into his legs he could, without attempting to, fly into the air about as high as a person's head and then gradually come down. With a little effort he could again rise as before. There is no way of expressing how much fun it was.

As he approached the temple gate he saw a crowd of people. Wondering what could be going on, he entered the gate, and there were red poppies in full bloom as far as one could see. He felt better than ever before. His dead father was standing amidst the flowers and asked, "Have you come too?" While somehow answering this, he went on. The boy he had lost earlier was there and also asked, "Papa, have you come too?" Matsunojo drew closer saying, "Is this where you have been?" The child said, "You can't come now!" At that moment someone by the gate called out his name loudly. As troublesome as it was, he paused reluctantly, and with a heavy heart, decided to turn back. Then he regained his senses. His relatives had gathered around, and were throwing water on him, to call him back to life. (1975, 68–69)

Even though this is not a first-person account, it is easily recognized as what is today called a "near-death experience." Although the cultural details of the temple and other aspects of local landscape make this unmistakably Japanese, the experiential features are universal. We do not need the term "out of body experience" to understand Matsunojo Kikuchi's ability to rise up in the air, any more than the context prevents us from recognizing the almost universal element of being told that it is not time for death.

Our understanding of cross-cultural patterns in narratives and beliefs about the supernatural is only beginning to take into account the non-ordinary experiences to which they often refer. Such an understanding will enrich our appreciation both of the distinctive qualities of cultures around the world and the common humanity of those who create, maintain, and live within them. Michiko Iwasaka and Barre Toelken's *Ghosts and the Japanese* is a very important and enjoyable step forward in this process.

Preface

In spite of a growing interest among Westerners to understand and analyze Japan and the Japanese—much of it sparked by rapidly developing business connections—what largely animates and informs the "Japaneseness" they seek to fathom actually lies where they do not look. People are reading everything possible (and impossible) about Japan that they can lay their hands on. Yet this eager pursuit seems one-dimensional, since people tend to seek answers only in particular directions, guided by their own (or someone else's) preconceptions, such as when they focus only on Confucianism, or Zen Buddhism, those impressive façades of Japan's culture which fascinate and impress Europeans and Americans as exotic and deeply meaningful.

Meaningful they certainly are, but in mistaking the façade for the building, the Westerner is often joined, unfortunately, by many of the Japanese themselves, who may not know their own culture very fully, or who find it profitable to advertise their country in the exotic terms so attractive to outsiders. Quite apart from the Confucian ethic, or the Zen Buddhist art of self-control, both of which have become something of a trademark for Japan's business success, there are many far more basic elements of vernacular culture, lived out in the experiences of everyday people, which constitute basic Japanese attitudes toward life and death, toward family, toward individual responsibility and deportment, and toward society.

As we have tried to illustrate in this book, these basic elements are found abundantly in the ongoing traditions and customs through which Japanese people articulate their relationships to each other and the world around them. In every culture, traditional expressions incorporate these important cultural elements of meaning, or else they would die out; thus recurrent topics and themes are valuable means to help an outsider perceive something about the insider's cultural values. For the Japanese, for example, one of the most persistent arenas of cultural concern through the ages has been death and its impact on everyday life. If our fresh look at Japanese death legends can give new readers a fuller sense of everyday culture in Japan, along with the opportunity and encouragement to reflect on the differences among cultures and their meanings generally, then we will be exceedingly pleased and well compensated for our efforts.

We would like to express our sincere thanks to those who have helped us to understand and articulate the complex dimensions of Japanese death lore in both contemporary life and historical retrospect: to Japanologists Klaus Antoni (University of Trier) and Stephen Kohl (University of Oregon), we owe particular insights into the relationships between older custom and modern cultural expression; folklorists Pack Carnes, Bruce Jackson, W. K. McNeil, and David Hufford provided extensive suggestions for examples and clarification; conversations with Yoko Elsner, Seiko Kikuta, Asako Marumoto, Akiko Tohmatsu, and Kanako Shiokawa helped us better understand the range of contemporary feeling and attitudes toward death among Japanese people. Midori and Kaori Ikematsu and Machiko Iwasaka established our first contacts with the monks of the Zenshōan Temple in Tokyo, where more than fifty portraits of ghosts are displayed yearly at Obon time.

We gratefully acknowledge the generous permission of the Kadokawa Shoten Publishing Co., Ltd., to quote from their massive folklore encyclopedia, *Nihon Minzokushi Taikei* (Tokyo: 1975); particular references are provided in the notes.

Much of our research would have been quite impossible without the friendly help of Dr. Andrée Belleville, Swiss specialist in Japanese Studies who was teaching German at Mie University. In response to our needs, she searched Japanese libraries and antique book stores for many of the works used in this study. Her skilled efforts enormously mitigated our problematic working distance from Japan.

Over the past thirteen years as the legend texts were translated and retranslated, and the chapters went through interminable revisions via overseas mail (Iwasaka lives in Germany, Toelken in Utah; their common language is German), several valiant typists learned more about Japanese customs than they had bargained for; for their patience, skill, and exceptional good cheer, we want to thank Susan Fagan at the University of Oregon, and Karen Krieger and Barbara Walker of Utah State University—the latter especially for her unfailing editorial insights and monumental good sense. Haruko Iwasaka generously supplied the calligraphy for the book.

Finally, a chance remark by a Tokyo taxicab driver led us to the Zenshōan Temple, near Ueno Park. Zenshōan, a Zen Buddhist temple, was founded in the Taitō-ku district of Tokyo in 1883 by Yamaoka Tesshū (1836–1888) for the purpose of praying for the spirits of those who had lost their lives during the Meiji Restoration. Yamaoka was a confidant of the last Tokugawa Shogun, Yoshinobu, and when the shogunate returned power to the emperor, Yamaoka was chosen to be the court's lord chamberlain. Among other assignments, he was put in charge of educating and training the young Emperor Meiji (1872–82). Famous as a swordsman, Yamaoka Tesshū founded a school of fencing and was also well known for his calligraphy. Although he never became a Buddhist priest, Yamaoka associated himself with Zenshōan during his final years, and his remains are buried in the temple's graveyard.

In addition to Yamaoka, a number of other prominent artists and politicians are interred at Zenshōan, among them the *rakugo* master, Sanyūtei Enchō (1839–1900). Enchō (born Isubuchi Jirōkichi), was the son of another *rakugo* artist, Tachibanaya Entarō, and made his first appearance on the *rakugo* stage when he was seven, under the stage name Koenta. At his mother's urging, he was apprenticed to a businessman and again later to the artist Utagawa Kuniyoshi, but both efforts were interrupted by poor health.

The boy eventually dedicated his life to the art of *rakugo*, a stage presentation of engaging narratives in which the artist takes the roles of all the characters, using variations in vocal tone and employing a fan, a kerchief, and other everyday items as evocative props. When he was seventeen, he took his stage name, Sanyūtei (the name of his artistic school) Enchō, and when he was twenty, he wrote his first *rakugo* piece—a *kaidan*, a story of the supernatural—and performed it. Composing many of the stories which he performed, he became one of the best known and most popular *rakugo* artists in the country—so much so that fans even emulated his hair style.

Later in life he studied Zen philosophy with Yamaoka Tesshū, and associated himself with the Zenshōan Temple, where he performed ghost stories each year during the Obon season. To this day, the custom is being observed, as master storytellers gather at the Zenshōan to tell supernatural tales at Obon. Enchō's private collection of more than fifty ghost portraits—which he had gathered for his study of ghost gestures and themes to be used in his works—was bequeathed to Zenshōan Temple at his death; they are exhibited each year during August, the Obon season. The pictures which accompany this book are a selection from that collection.

At the Zenshōan, we were kindly allowed to survey the temple's extensive collection of ghost pictures, and subsequently we were permitted to reproduce those we found appropriate for this book. We would like to express our gratitude to Reverend Genkyo Hirai (recently deceased) and the monks of Zenshōan for their hospitality and cooperation, and for their permission to use pictures from their treasury. Travel expenses to do research at the Zenshōan Temple as well as support for the publication costs of reproducing the ghost portraits were generously supplied by Brian Pitcher, dean of the College of Humanities, Arts, and Social Sciences at Utah State University.

幽霊と日本人

Part I

An Introduction to the Left Stairway

Of the many popular stereotypes about Japan, two of the most common are curiously in opposition. One, based on current successes in business and finance, depicts the Japanese as narrowly ethnocentric and internationally aggressive, and sees their behavior as a holdover from the samurai era. In this view, Japanese business leaders are feudal lords who have only thinly disguised their true identity by shifting from kimono and sword to three-piece suit and computer. One approaches a business meeting with them using the same delicate caution associated with visiting a daimyo in his castle. Americans who want to initiate relationships with Japan study Zen Buddhism, samurai behavior, and elite pastimes ranging from archery to flower arranging. From this perspective, the Japanese system is perceived as pervasive, monolithic, unavoidable; we read phrases like "The Japanese believe..." and "Japanese businessmen always..." and "When in Japan, you must never...." This stereotype represents Japan as having changed little since olden times, as a country which maintains an aggressive stance toward other cultures' land, money, and property.

As with all stereotypes, this one may contain a grain of accuracy; for instance, the very powerful *uchi/soto* (insider/outsider) considerations which animate much Japanese corporate activity probably informed samurai behavior as well, and the foreign observer may simply be mistaking a certain popular historical model for an ongoing process. The real error of the stereotype is the conclusion that all Japan runs on a single, deep-level system of belief and behavior. The much touted *uchi/soto* distinction, which may indeed provide a foundation for judgment and action, is found throughout the world, and even in Japan, it is not encountered under all circumstances or in the same way. And it does not account for a myriad of other significant phenomena which one meets daily on the streets, at work, or in conversation. Clearly many other cultural processes are at work.

Even the casual visitor to Japan will notice after a few days that the visible aspects of everyday custom and traditional behavior do not fit into one monolithic system. Typically the same family that uses a Shintō ceremony for weddings will observe Buddhist rites for funerals; a businessman who espouses Confucian precepts in his profession may be a practicing Christian, a nonchalant Buddhist, or—perhaps most often—a member of no religion at all. Eventually, if the visitor is not confused by this amalgam, the Japanese will emerge as a people who have been able to adopt, adapt, translate, reform, and integrate the ideas and values of many cultures and religions into their own system.

While this cultural dynamism and eagerness to absorb may not impede our study of Japanese art, religion, philosophy, and written language, they often deeply affect our ability to understand more recent developments in Japan and lead directly to the second popular stereotype: the Japanese have become too "Westernized." They have neon lights, computers, television, transistors, Kleenex, automobiles, a Disneyland, and Kentucky Fried Chicken. Without pausing to wonder whether the Japanese may have invented some of these items themselves, and instead accepting another of our favorite preconceptions that the Japanese are always "copying" things which originated elsewhere, we visitors may easily conclude that the "old Japan" no longer survives because its graceful cherry-blossom viewers have been replaced by rude, ambitious throngs of office workers who cram themselves suicidally into modern trains running at 200 percent capacity. The geisha has given way to the bowing department-store zombie, we think, and the samisen has been blasted off the stage by karaoke and the electric guitar. Japan is not what our romantic stereotypes have prepared us to expect: couples are now married in New England-style churches (often on package tours to Hawaii), and picturesque farm houses display a forest of television antennas which spoil our scenic photos. So much for the wonderful, artistic, "authentic" Japanese way of life, we lament, forgetting that similar changes in our own culture do not puzzle us at all and that a few years ago, we were at war with these people whose culture was then considered unalterably alien, unfathomable, and frightening.

We are also inclined to overlook in both of these stereotypes that the most meaningful and enduring parts of a culture may not be its most visible or conscious ones. A complex of shared cultural values animates much of what can and cannot happen in Japan, and these are seldom consciously articulated even though they can be experienced daily on the street.

For example, the outsider often becomes a part of dodging games when encountering Japanese pedestrians, or worse, finds himself on the wrong (that is to say, right-hand) side of a public stairway. Americans or Europeans will try to exit a subway during rush hour by sticking doggedly and "properly" to the right-hand railing while being carried grimly and unremittingly back down the stairs by what is surely half of Tokyo's population. The Japanese, if they notice what is happening at all, do not speak or apologize. In fact, they may glare briefly at the unfortunate *gaijin* who has again managed to get into the wrong place and is inconveniencing and embarrassing several thousand Japanese citizens who deserve something better than crude idiosyncrasy in crowded places.

A Japanese person walking alone in this crowd would normally move to the left (for the same reason an American would move to the right) because it is customary, especially at rush hour, when space is limited and people are in a hurry. The flow of the larger group is not impeded, and the individual—by conforming to the group dynamic—reaches the goal without difficulty. Indeed, in some Tokyo subway stations where foreigners are most likely to appear, there are now footprints painted on the floor to indicate the way to the correct stairway or escalator.

When walking together in groups (among friends, relatives, business colleagues), however, Japanese pedestrians, like those in other countries, seem to use another model; the group, moving together like a bubble in the larger stream, may take up an entire sidewalk or stairway, regardless of who else—Japanese or *gaijin*—may be coming in the opposite direction and keeping properly to the left. In this case, the group exerts a right-of-way (a kind of cultural easement) over others in the stream, often forcing them into the street or up against the wall. After spending a year in Japan trying to figure out these movement patterns, Professor Stephen Kohl of the University of Oregon decided that "walking in Japan is a full-body contact sport"; an unwary foreigner might be inclined to describe them as life threatening if encountered under rushed and stressful circumstances.

Yet the Japanese model (if there is one) is no more threatening in and of itself than the American one; neither practice is obstinate or contrary or arrogant. At the same time, neither one can be clearly and unequivocally articulated by those for whom the pattern is "normal." Both systems are relatively consistent, and both are based on doing what feels right according to assumptions which, though seldom openly stated, are so deeply integrated into the values and actions of everyday life that they do not require conscious thought. Anthropologist Edward T. Hall has suggested that because these cultural values are so basic to our sense of normality, and because we do not deal with them consciously, we often become aware of them only when someone threatens us by acting "abnormally." The anxiety or anger which results may be demonstrated by glares on the Japanese subway staircase, or in physical actions like those of a well-dressed woman who encountered the coauthor of this book during Christmas season, walking on the left side of a German sidewalk, and thrashed her with an umbrella, yelling, "Shameless! Shameless! In Germany, we walk in the right place!"

Every culture which remains alive is well supplied with these codes of everyday behavior and value, along with attendant emotions, regardless of how many other philosophies it may have borrowed and how literate and sophisticated its members may be. America has thousands of these customs of cultural and social communication, and so has

Japan. Usually our customs are learned by example (or by consistent omission) and through the stories, jokes, anecdotes, remarks, and actions of those closest to us as we are forming our concepts of normality, that is, from our families. Such ideas and values remain unstated and unquestioned most of the time because they represent self-evident, usual ways of behaving; they are quickly mentioned, however, if we transgress the unstated rule, when we suddenly hear a parent thunder, "Don't ever let me catch you doing that again!" These, then, are the least likely subjects to come up when we consciously or intellectually discuss our culture or that of others: when was the last time you talked about which side of the staircase your culture uses, or how close you stand to a stranger of the opposite sex while conversing, or the cultural variations in the meaning of eye contact?

Reaching and recognizing this dynamic and underlying level of cultural communication can be one of the most exciting adventures, though, for we suddenly find windows opening up, lights going on, things making sense that were previously clouded, confusing, or even seemed dangerous. We begin to watch for the unspoken, the automatic, the "obvious"; for the patterned ways in which things do or do not happen; and for the subtle and unmentioned "normalities" that lie at the heart of the familiar—and thus enduring and sustaining—parts of everyday life. Figuratively speaking, we should be willing to experience both sides of the stairway, to become aware of the familiar (as obvious and simple as that may sound) in such a way that cultural practices different from our own will register as adventures in the kaleidoscope of human meaning rather than confirmation that other peoples are crude or backward.

Many are unwilling to go this far, and perhaps do not even consider it an alternative. A friend of ours, an American woman long familiar with Japan and its language, confided that after her first year in Tokyo, she could not take the daily beating any longer and exchanged her soft leather handbag for a hard-shell briefcase—the better to protect herself from subway crowds. She is still convinced, years later, that the Japanese at rush hour simply suspend the norms of human consideration, and would even ignore the Geneva Convention to reach their trains on time. We believe the truth is—embarrassingly—far simpler: she probably never considered that the *left* side of the stairway was a normal place to walk.

It is not with the aim of helping businessmen or tourists to avoid embarrassment in the subway, but in the hopes of suggesting where people might find the right (left) side of the Japanese *cultural* stairway (and be willing to consider using it) that we have put this book together. Since the everyday codes are so numerous, however, we have decided to focus on one area of great interest and significance in modern Japan (as well as in times past), yet one which people do not generally articulate in spite of the anxieties, fascinations and routine avoidances prompted by it. It is a subject now widely discussed among psychologists as well as folklorists and anthropologists: death and dying, and includes all the culturally interpreted interfaces between the world in which we live (*kono-yo*) and the world beyond (*ano-yo*), most obviously, of course, ghosts and spirits.

Our impression, after having worked on this project for some thirteen years, is that death is not only a common subject in Japanese folklore but seems indeed to be the *principal* topic in Japanese tradition; nearly every festival, every ritual, every custom is bound up in some way with relationships between the living and the dead, between the present family and its ancestors, between the present occupation and its forebears. We would venture the hypothesis that death is the prototypical Japanese topic, not only because it relates living people to their ongoing heritage, but also— as the legends we've selected show—because death brings into focus a number of other very important elements in the Japanese worldview: obligation, duty, debt, honor, and personal responsibility.

For Europeans and Americans, death has been until recently a relatively touchy subject, one that is not publicly very popular or comfortable. In *Le Vieillesse*, Simone de Beauvoir shows how repugnant the topic has been in Europe. To get old, to decompose, to disappear from the scene are realities that many Westerners have had trouble confronting. And yet, since the Middle Ages, there has been as well a macabre fascination with death in literature and art. Fear and apprehension about it are found in Asia as well, the difference being the varied ways in which death can be viewed; thus, in Japan, death can be a symbol of the transience of life, although the soul is perceived as not transitory; death even constitutes a kind of aesthetic, in spite of one's abhorrence of the process; it can inform a sort of romanticism, especially as expressed in the Edo Period (one finds it even

A standard depiction of a woman's ghost. Artist: Maruyama Ōkyo (1733–1795).

today). Nonetheless, in their everyday lives, the Japanese assiduously avoid unlucky words or numbers suggestive of death; clearly a dialectic tension exists between the philosophical and the everyday perceptions of death, and these contradictions and ambiguities are given narrative form in the legends.

Besides being dramatizations of fear, uncertainty, and ambiguity, the legends richly illustrate a worldview in which the realms of the living and the dead interpenetrate in a system of mutual responsibility. While trying to avoid any suggestion of death in daily conversation, a typical Japanese will be constantly involved with funerals and anecdotes and legends and family obligations which continually keep the topic alive. It can be said without exaggeration that the Japanese busy themselves with death their whole lives long.

As the legends vividly illustrate, and as Yanagita Kunio pointed out in his influential book *About Our Ancestors*, the traditional Japanese world of the dead lies not far from the world of the living, and the souls of departed relatives remain among the survivors, or at least close enough to visit the family during Obon season, for example. Also their world, the world of the dead, remains "alive," even after death in this world has occurred. This attitude toward death, and human relationships with those who have passed on to the other world, is originally based on neither Neo-Confucianism nor Buddhism, but rather on the much earlier "ancestor cult" (or "ancestor complex," as Professor Yamashita Shinji has more recently called it). This Shintō-based ancestor complex, which had already been in place for a thousand years by the time of the Tokugawa era, characterizes the whole Japanese social structure, even if it is not consciously recognized or intellectually articulated.

The origin of the much discussed Japanese family system also lies within this set of values and is further reflected in the character of practically every institution, including modern corporations. Knowing something about the ancestor system allows anyone, Japanese or not, to read the culture from the inside out, rather than starting with the façade and trying to guess what lies behind it.

Many of the legends we include in this book were published in a journal devoted to Japanese and East Asian folklore, *Tabi to Densetsu* (Travel and Legend), between 1928 and 1932 by various collectors. In these first years of publication, the journal did not present the legends as separate, discrete texts with explanatory notes, but rather mentioned them in connection with essays on broader themes and topics, often elliptically, but sometimes with surrounding commentary on the context and occasion. Since this is the way legends usually appear in conversation—as illustrations of larger issues such as the nature of spirits, the return of the dead, and so on—we have also tried to present them without decoration, adding only what may be necessary to allow the reader a fuller understanding of the story and its possible meanings. This book thus does not pretend to offer a full collection of Japanese death legends, but rather a selection of a few culturally typical narratives which illustrate some of the Japanese assumptions about the nature of death.

The stories themselves give us a dramatized view of many customs, legends, tales, and the like which were still in wide use before World War II. The choice of legends from this era is deliberate: for one thing, this was the high point of early Japanese field collecting, and thus the narratives constitute the first extensive body of folk materials collected intentionally from oral tradition by folklorists in Japan. As well, they provide us with a range of narratives which were common in Japan prior to the time when Westerners became interested in Japanese culture. Since World War II, we have known Japan better (comparatively), and have become more familiar with some Japanese themes through translated novels and poems, the arts, and films, even though we have simultaneously concluded that Japan is now solidly Westernized. These legends from the 1920s and 1930s supply a link between the present and the relatively distant past (which we can still perceive at least partially through earlier Japanese writings and the world of wood-block prints) and indicate that our Westernization model—while it may describe part of the façade—does not account for the persistence of deeper and older aspects of Japanese culture.

While many of the particular legends may have died out of oral tradition in the meanwhile, other similar ones have developed; clearly, as in the folklore of all societies, the details and current interests may change continually, but the culturally important themes and issues remain. For this reason, we have also referred to legends collected more recently. Still, the interested reader would do well to read far beyond this book, especially into the research of contemporary Japanese folklorists, which is slowly becoming more available. And, even better, those with language capability should try encountering the stories alive, in their natural habitats among the everyday people of Japan.

The particular legend texts we've used are colored by other factors not under our control; for one thing, they were collected from people in all parts of Japan by folklorists who wrote down the stories as best they could, some of them no doubt catching the original wording and nuances better than others. In addition, certain beliefs and customs vary from one part of Japan to another, and the same story or legend may well have local meanings which the collector did not understand and which we can no longer find out about. Still further, many of these stories are told with a logic which suggests that Buddhism or Shintōism or Confucianism may have co-opted or adapted the text over the course of time; a legend, for example, which might have represented an entirely local ancestor complex may have been rationalized later to illustrate filial piety; a story about a dead mother's concern for her coffin-born child may be told in one province to demonstrate the need for Buddhist sutras and in another to warn about the ritual danger of a dead fetus. In all cases, the beliefs and reactions of the collectors, their own notions about what the legend might mean, may have played a part in the way they conveyed the text to their reading audiences.

Still other details of immediate context—though of central importance to the ultimate meaning of any text—are simply not given in the originals. A folklorist or ethnographer collecting these legends today would feel it important to note where a narrator laughed or an audience gasped, where gestures were made and how they were received, where certain words or phrases were puzzling or particularly pleasing to the audience. That is because the living texture of performance as it proceeds from the immediate context of narration is a part of the meaning of the text—at least provisionally. If the actions of a particular character are obviously stupid or unnatural, if a certain gesture or word is archaic or out of place, if a certain term is impolite or ironically used, the narrator and the audience will register that in the live context—even though no specific words to indicate it may enter the text. Since many of the legends in this book were elicited from rural people by scholars doing research, however, we can suspect that in many cases the live performance was not identical to the narrations that would have occurred among the people on their own.

For these reasons, there are multiple possibilities here for misunderstanding, limited appreciation of meaning, or impaired reception of a clear cultural picture. We have tried to account for as many of the central issues as we can, working from a generalized knowledge of familiar themes and motifs in Japanese folklore, but the important dimension of immediate performance context remains for the most part unknowable.

Even so, in our treatment of these customs and legends, we want as much as possible to stress their live, performative aspect, because these are cultural expressions which *normally* continue to exist because they are performed by people among themselves, not read about in books. Of course, there persists a dynamic dialectic between the printed page and contemporary culture, between formal and informal, between "elite" and "folk," between consciously learned and unconsciously absorbed expressions; it would be strange if it were not so. But the oral component of any culture, that part which is maintained in the mundane, out-of-awareness grind of everyday life and cultural normality, is the element that most deeply animates the culture and its range of understood meanings—even though it is so normal and everyday that we seldom take the effort to look at it—or hear it—analytically. Thus we have chosen some fossils as examples, but we are really talking about the *living* system they belong to—even though the topic is death.

The ghost of a decadent monk who was turned into the spirit of Gaki (one of the least fortunate Buddhist categories in the afterlife). Artist: Gyōshin (other information unknown).

Part II

Death Customs in Contemporary Japan

It is abundantly clear to anyone interested in Japanese culture that the performative media—theatre, Kabuki, film, and storytelling (such as the *kaidan banashi* recitals)—are well stocked with stories which feature death, ghosts, *oni*, and other monsters, and which include the same emotions of revenge, fury, obligation, and frustration that figure centrally as motivations in the folk legends. A favorite among the many topics which form the content of these productions, death and anything connected to it continue to strike a responsive and meaningful chord in Japanese audiences. On the level of interest, popularity, and intellectual involvement of artists, death is foregrounded in performances which dramatize issues of enduring validity in Japanese society.

But death is more than a simple topic of intellectual interest: when we hear that a modern film director has visited the Tokyo gravesite of Oiwa before daring to make a film about her tortuous death and grim revenge; when we learn that actors and stagehands in the Kabuki theatre perform a ceremony to prevent bad luck and accidents which might occur during the enactment of Oiwa's story or that of Kiku (the servant girl who killed herself over breaking an expensive porcelain plate); when we find out that storytellers are concerned about the possible misfortune which may result from relating particular ghost stories; when we discover that Tokyo taxi drivers still talk about transporting ghosts—then we realize that something more deep and pervasive than academic interest is involved.

There are at least five important observations to derive from these revelations: (1) the seemingly older idea of ghostly revenge has been transported into modern situations and incorporated into everyday practice; (2) beliefs about one's personal responsibility with respect to ghosts are still functional—even in the relatively "liberated" world of the contemporary performer; (3) the "verisimilitude" an actor adopts when assuming a traditional role is based on another—perhaps more real and personal—kind of logic than in Western culture (although there are parallel beliefs and taboos about Shakespeare's plays among American thespians); (4) legends and their ghostly referents remain powerful and potentially dangerous through time; (5) the Land of the Dead is still thought to be nearby.

Similar observations can be made about modern fiction. For example, in Kawabata Yasunari's short story "Fushi" (Beyond death), the two characters are the ghost of a beautiful young woman and an old man—her surviving lover—who dies during the story as they walk along recounting what separated them and led to her suicide. The logic or sense of verisimilitude in such a story is beyond the comprehension of a Western reader, as is the central issue of Kawabata's story "Tabi," in which a young girl recalls a red hat and white *tabi* being put into the casket of a dead teacher. Abe Kōbō's "Shinda musume ga utatta..." (Song of a dead girl) is narrated in the first person by a young woman whose suicide takes place on the very first page; it is her ghost through whom we vicariously experience and recall the frustrating events of her limited life. In Hiraiwa Yumie's "Yūgao no onna" (Lady of the evening faces), the unfolding of the first part of the story relates directly to the seventh-, forty-ninth-, and hundredth-day funeral observances by the main character for her departed mother. Not surprisingly, the young woman becomes involved in a "dead" marriage, but manages to extricate herself through the same kind of solitary personal strength which brought her through the difficulties of her mother's demise.

It seems that the same drive to experience a personal interaction with the mysteries and realities of the "other side" which motivated audiences in earlier times to flock to performances of the *One Hundred Tales* (during which it was believed someone in the audience might die before the hundredth story was told and the hundredth—and last—candle was extinguished) still draws people to modern rephrasings of the same cluster of values. Just as Fosco Maraini, in *Japan: Patterns of Continuity*, argues from visual evidence that older Japanese concepts continue to be rearticulated in modern media and experience, so it seems that a deep level of culture finds reexpression and rephrasing in modern oral forms as well.

But what are the values that are represented by these articulations? What are the assumptions about death and the human spirit that reach concrete or dramatic reality through vehicles like legend, belief, and custom? Obviously the topic is deeper and more complex than a brief study can encompass; nonetheless, Japanese folklorists and anthropologists have given us some good maps which lead into the territory, and we can explore them profitably by using careful observations of ongoing customs and legends as guideposts.

For example, we can infer something about the nature and location of the recently departed spirit by noting the custom, once widespread in Japan (and still found in many areas), of calling out the name of the just-deceased, sometimes from the rooftop, for a period of time after his or her death. Apparently the spirit does not go far, and may be ready to come back. Indeed the Japanese terms associated with the spatial aspects of the spirit's location are based on the standard positional markers: *ko* (here, this side), *so* (there, intermediate distance), and *a* (over yonder, behind, the other side). *Konoyo*, "this world here," is the precinct of the living; *anoyo*, "the world over there, yonder" is clearly the other side, the long-term abode of the dead (note that there is no ambiguous middle ground called *sonoyo*; the dichotomy is clearly drawn). From "over there," the spirit still retains a connection with and interest in the affairs of "this world," for as it develops slowly into the local collective ancestral deity called *sorei* and *kami*, it remains concerned about family identity, survival, and welfare.

But before the spirit gets all the way to *anoyo*, which can take up to forty-nine days, it may be called back; unfinished business, unfulfilled obligations, a need for vengeance, feelings of jealousy, the desire for proper burial or more ritual, and the like may impede the spirit's progress and keep it in the *konoyo* zone, where it will appear in the form of a ghost or cemetery fires or other striking phenomena. Understanding the legends in this book requires the reader/listener to understand and accept the values which are thought to keep a soul in this zone until a problem is properly resolved. In other words, it is not enough simply to acknowledge that the Japanese may believe in ghosts; ghosts are thought to express certain dilemmas which require culturally acceptable solutions. It is the values represented by these problems and reflected in their resolutions that the legends dramatize.

The concept of *anoyo*, moreover, is not only literal but also metaphorical, for there are apparently a variety of "places" where spirits are thought to go on to. "The world over yonder" is said by some to be far away over the sea; for others, it is past the mountains; for others, it lies beyond a great river; and in the *Kojiki*, it is described as being underground. Some of these variations may be accounted for by the possibility that the beliefs in southern Japan were influenced by Polynesian cultures from "far away over the sea," while many other cultural streams came into Japan from Mongolia via Korea, and the topography—plus Japan's own mountains, which cover between eighty and ninety percent of the land mass—would account for the prominence of mountain imagery. Earlier local beliefs may well have been associated with particular lakes and streams which were thought to have their own power. Later additions, rationalizations, and reinterpretations by Buddhist, Confucian, and Shintō commentators have certainly complicated this mixture theologically, but the practical, everyday application of the concept can still be heard in the terms *konoyo* and *anoyo*. The "yonder" world in almost all cases is final, and entry into it is preceded, for guilty persons, by some kind of judgment and punishment (which can be modified or softened by the sutras read on their behalf at the request of the survivors, according to more recent belief).

What seems to interest the Japanese imagination is the idea that the soul tends to stay somewhere close to *konoyo* if there is anything which binds it to this life: mostly this will not be a theological situation but a cultural one, in which the

The ghost of a blind musician crossing a river. Artist: Andō Hiroshige (1797–1858).

spirit's orderly transition is dependent on finishing a task or fulfilling a culturally valid obligation. Dramatically speaking, then, the legend character who is confronted by a ghost who needs help to resolve an unfinished task is cast in the role of an observer or witness to the existence of both worlds interacting, as well as a living testimony to the validity of the resolution.

It may not always be possible for the character in the story (much less the listener) to determine at once what kind of ghost he or she has encountered. For one thing, there are two kinds of spirits: those from living persons, where a spirit has left a body momentarily but the person remains alive (no doubt this would be called a "near-death experience" in current parlance, but it is also thought to be caused by severe anger, a trance, or anxiety), and those from genuinely dead persons. The former are called *seiryō* or *shōryō* (and are amply dramatized in such works as *The Tales of Genji* and *Konjaku Monogatari*); the latter—which we deal with mainly in this study—are called *shiryō*.

Beyond that, the legend character may not be able to tell what kind of help would aid the dead spirit which is "trapped" on this side of the great boundary. Lucky for the character if the ghost can articulate a request that the witness can then fulfill; in many cases, the witness is an innocent passerby who is simply assaulted by a ghost whose uncontrollable passion results from the way he died, or the fact that the proper rituals were not observed in her behalf. But from the Japanese perspective, the apparently innocent victim may not be entirely exempt from involvement, for he or she is a member of the living, that group of people whose *obligation* it is to celebrate the souls of the dead. In this dramatic sense, anyone alive is fair game for the approach of a ghost.

What is there in Japanese cultural values, though, that has the power to keep spirits from moving to the other side, that justifies furious ghost attacks on living persons, that accounts for a dead mother nursing a living baby? The term *on*, with all its attendant implications, supplies one possible answer. *On* translates into something like "obligation" or "responsibility," but it is infinitely more complicated, and colored with such a range of cultural attitudes and assumptions that a single, clear definition is impossible to articulate in either Japanese or English. Technically, *on* is the kind of obligation one assumes (in the Japanese idiom, one *wears* it) when one has been the recipient of love, nurturance, kindness, favor, help, or advice—especially from a superior in the social system. *On* entails not only an awareness of having received a favor, but carries with it the absolute necessity to respond and repay. Some kinds of *on* debt, called *giri*, can be repaid in kind, or with work, money, or gifts which are in some way equal to the original favor. But the most difficult and far-reaching debts inhere in family relationships: within the immediate family, in terms of filial piety to one's own parents; in the "vertical" family of ancestors and descendants; in the social systems (village, occupational) which are modeled on the framework of the family; in the relationship to the emperor, father of the culture (who, incidentally, "wears" his *on* to his own ancestors and to the *kami*). No one is exempt, and this familial *on*, in which the debt is called *gimu*, can never be fully repaid; Ruth Benedict says of it, "The fullest repayment of these obligations is still no more than partial, and there is no time limit" (1946, 116).

Each person has received so much in nurturance and help from others that one is always in a state of debt, and this is especially so among those who share an *uchi* (insider) relationship, which may range from an immediate family to a large corporation. By the same token, one expects to help others and bestow *on* upon them through love, concern, favors, and the like. Thus everyone up and down the social system experiences a keen sense of obligation. Since the system itself is a complex of status relationships (some of which may be fixed and others born of situation and context), one never has the sense of being caught up on all the debt; one always lives with an apologetic acknowledgment of being unequal and behind in one's "payments."

When a debt to another is not paid, people on both sides of the transaction may feel guilty, insulted, or outraged. Thus not only does the occasional act of doing a real or imagined wrong to another require apology and discussion, but also the omitted act of obligation may be interpreted as an outright injury. And because of all the potential imbalances in the situation, even doing someone a good turn may create such an obligation that an apology is necessary. The Japanese spend a good deal of time apologizing to each other for matters which would seem more positive than negative to an outsider.

Almost anyone who dies will expire, then, with many unfulfilled obligations to others, and the relatives of that person will also be aware that they still have many obligations to the deceased. The resultant paroxysm of guilt and apology can be articulated and directed to some extent by the survivors' commitment to the proper rituals, complete with the reading of sutras and offering of food. The recourse available to the deceased is, according to the legends at least, the possibility of remaining in the vicinity until the principal inequities have been redressed. The ghost may simply want more sutras read, or may feel the need for something more specific. If the deceased has been wrongfully treated, consciously injured, murdered, insulted, or the like, the ghost may wreak vengeance on the wrongdoer—or by extension, the culprit's family, clan, village, or region, even for generations (just as there are no time limits for the debt to be paid, there are also none for some kinds of vengeance).

In literary terms, it is nearly irrelevant whether people actually believe a spirit can return, or if the ghosts are "simply" the public dramatizations of guilt felt by survivors: the ghost legends are powerful expressions of the obligations and niceties which the Japanese feel are incumbent upon themselves as they lead normal, acceptable lives within their culture. The outcome is the same in either case, for these legends ensure the kind of behavior which preserves the culture and its values, along with the proper relationships without which—in the Japanese view—culture would be meaningless.

The ritualization of these relationships and obligations can be seen vividly in Japanese funeral ceremonies. Originally Buddhism had no funeral as such, for the teaching of Buddha concentrates on the search for an understanding of the meaning in life and thus has little to do with death. As Buddhism came to Japan by way of China, the land of ancestor cults, it became slowly involved with ancestor veneration and was well received in Japan where ancestral deities were worshipped. But it appears that people in those days abhorred death and tried to avoid any contact with dead bodies, since death generically and dead bodies in particular were considered unclean and impure. Early Japanese simply disposed of the corpses where they could, or placed them aside without any ceremony at all.

Moreover, there is no evidence that the earliest Buddhist monks or temples concerned themselves with death or funeral ceremonies. Not until the Heian Period (the end of the eighth century to the beginning of the twelfth century), during a great famine in which countless corpses littered the streets and were being eaten by animals and birds, did the monks bury people and read sutras for them out of Buddhist compassion. This seems to mark the beginning of funeral practices among the monks, and since that time, the Buddhist monks have been especially prominent in funeral rituals. At first, it appears that temples were built near the places where many people had been buried, so that the sutras could be more conveniently read for them; in later times, the custom of taking the deceased to a place where a temple was already located developed. Cemeteries within temple precincts, such as those described in many of our legends, are thus relatively recent.

Since the original religion of Japan considered death as unclean, the development of cemeteries took an interesting turn, for people began to erect two separate graves: one as the actual place where the corpse was interred, which no one would visit after the burial, the other as a memorial spot where family members would meet regularly and celebrate their ancestors. Today, since corpses are usually cremated, one grave is the rule.

But the complicated funeral practices developed by the Buddhists speak to the prior existence in Japan of an extensive set of beliefs about ongoing relationships with the dead. Why would Buddhism develop the multiday and multiyear funeral system when in fact Buddhism taught that the dying person immediately becomes a Buddha (or, if guilty, a member of a lower order of beings)? Apparently the Buddhists appropriated and helped to develop an extremely complex system which already had existed, without the help of temple ritual, for eons—perhaps in much the same way that the early Christian church adopted and adapted itself to local "pagan" practices, personages, and holy places. Yanagita and others have pointed out a number of indications for an early ancestor complex, which apparently became the matrix for present-day practices that may look Buddhist but actually stem from an earlier period in Japan's cultural history. For this reason, Japanese Buddhism cannot be easily compared with other forms of the same religion, for it was deeply influenced by local customs.

The typical Buddhist funerals which are still celebrated in Japan were developed during the Edo Period (1603–1867), but are of course grounded on these older customs and concepts. Generally speaking (keeping in mind that in different areas there may be distinctive variations), the funeral consists of four primary areas of focus, plus other commemorations during subsequent years:

1. *Tsuya* (the wake), literally, "to pass the night." One night before the burial or cremation, family members and anyone else who had a particularly close relationship with the departed remain with the body all night. Silence is observed, though some occasional small conversation may take place. The family altar is usually decorated with flowers, and a Buddhist monk may read sutras to pacify and console the spirit of the deceased. Rice, fish, vegetables, and sake may be served to visitors.

Earlier, in some areas (like Nagaoka-gun in Kōchi-ken), it was called *tsuya* when people in a neighborhood met in a Shintō shrine and prayed for a sick person in critical condition. Later the *tsuya* developed into a prayer meeting for the recently deceased. In various areas, there was also the custom of siblings or other family members sleeping next to the corpse on the first night after death. Or a person who had recently lost a family member (within the previous year) and was thus still in mourning and considered ritually "unclean" would stay the first night in the same room with the corpse.

Food customs at the *tsuya* are also interesting, for what is offered to visitors at the wake varies according to region. Thus, though the overall funeral practice is standardized, the particulars of deportment and food selection help to foreground the local intensity with which both life and death are experienced. Apparently elements from various religious traditions have melded into a particularly Japanese funeral ceremony.

2. *Sōshiki* (the funeral). Today it is common for a mortuary firm (*sōgiya*) to construct a decorated altar in a room of the deceased's house (or in a hall, like a temple). The coffin is placed in the middle of this altar, which is constructed to look like a broad stair or raised platform. If the funeral is not Shintō, a Buddhist monk reads appropriate sutras on behalf of the deceased. Afterward each visitor goes forward to the altar, offers incense, and prays. After all have performed this ritual, men carry the coffin out of the house and put it into a hearse, which brings the corpse to the crematorium for burning. It is common nowadays for the closest family members not to accompany the corpse to the crematorium; instead they gather at a nearby restaurant for a catered meal.

A ghost performance on the Kabuki stage. Artist: Iijima Kōga (other information unknown).

The altar is dismantled by the mortuary and taken from the house.

The ashes of the deceased are preserved in an urn, the larger fragments of bone being passed from one pair of mixed chopsticks to another, and are kept on the household altar, accompanied by a small tablet with the person's name, until the forty-ninth day ceremony, after which the urn is placed in a grave. Every Japanese, with the exception of Christians and Jews, receives a so-called posthumous name (*kaimyō*), and it is this special name which appears on the funeral tablet (*ihai*).

Rural funerals often still include housecleaning, making of clothes for the deceased, and home preparation of food for guests. Frequently a *zuda-bukuro* (pilgrim's bag) is prepared by family members; into it go fingernail parings, personal articles (like a tobacco pipe), and a few imitation *mon*, an archaic coin also mentioned in a number of the legends, which will pay the spirit's fare on the ferry to *anoyo*. The bag is placed around the neck of the corpse before cremation.

3. *Shonanoka* (the seventh day after death). On this day, a special ceremony called *hōji* is held, during which sutras are read (either at home or in a nearby temple), based on the belief that the spirit of a person returns home on the seventh day after death. Among Buddhist Japanese-Americans, the "seventh-day" ceremony is held on the afternoon of the funeral since family members are so widely dispersed that a second gathering a week later is an inconvenience.

4. *Shijū-kunichi* (the forty-ninth day after death). The ceremony for the dead is also performed on this day, for after the forty-ninth day it is believed that the soul starts its new life "on the other side" (unless its progress has been slowed as already discussed). Between death in this world and the beginning of a new life in the afterworld, the soul has remained *konoyo*, somewhere in the vicinity of its home, where it should have been honored, pacified, and consoled.

Many of the particular ritual days following the funeral (and the precise number varies, including in some areas the fourteenth, twenty-first, twenty-eighth, thirty-fifth, and forty-second, in addition to or instead of those already mentioned) focus on the reading of particular sutras, the purpose of which is to lessen the possibilities for punishment faced by the deceased in passing to the other side. According to the Chinese sutra Jizō-jūō-kyō, the spirit of a dead person must face ten judges, one after another. On the seventh day after death, the deceased is brought before the first judge and closely questioned about how he has led his life. Then, on various key days like those above, he comes before the court again and again for nine more trials. On the forty-ninth day, the final verdict is handed down and the decision made as to which of six worlds (among them Hell, Animal, Insanity, Human, Heaven) the spirit must enter. The survivors, in order to obtain a milder sentence for the sinner (or to urge a pardon for someone who has received a heavy penalty), order sutras to be read. Even when a dead person has been consigned to heaven for having led a very good life, if the survivors neglect to have the sutras read, it can endanger his position and cause him to fall into hell anyway—at least according to the Jizō-jūō-kyō sutra.

After the immediate funeral arrangements have been taken care of, there remain the various important annual anniversaries of the death: the first, second, third, seventh, thirteenth, seventeenth, twenty-third or twenty-fifth, twenty-seventh, thirty-third, and occasionally the fiftieth and the hundredth (obviously these last are observed by descendants who probably did not know the deceased personally, but who feel an obligation to maintain proper filial relationships with the *kami* of their family). On each of these memorial days, a Buddhist priest may be engaged to read appropriate sutras in a ceremonial setting in a temple, or family members and close friends may gather at home and have them read there. Flowers and incense are offered on the family altar, and afterward a festive meal is shared.

Clearly such a calendar of events has the effect of organizing the life of a family over a period of years, and if several people in the family have died, it is not at all difficult to imagine much of the year devoted to fulfilling funeral obligations. In a context where considerations for the dead are so prominent, it is no wonder that death and many things related to it are such likely subjects for expression in narrative form; given the stress on unfulfillable obligations in family life, it is not surprising that an aura of guilt, unfinished business, and unfathomable debt permeates these stories and provides much of their characters' motivations. The ongoing beliefs and rituals connected with death, in concert with a deep-seated style of human interaction expressed in the *on* complex, surely create a rich and meaningful matrix for the ghost legends as a genre as well as for much of the everyday activity in a family as it makes its way through seemingly endless rituals.

At the same time, such an intense, ongoing concentration on the welfare of the dead, and the unbreakable responsibilities which relate the living to them, continually engages the dead in the lives of the living, and thus preserves the dead within the present day—much as Yanagita suggested. Kishimoto Hideo comments that "for the Japanese, death is within life." As long as we continue to ritualize the dead, they remain a part of our existence; although their spirits have presumably gone on, *anoyo*, some aspect of their personality, their function, their status (and thus the *on* that attaches to all of these) remains with us. As they slowly become *kami*, the local or national deities that bestow blessings, favors, and nurturance upon our affairs, we continue to make known the endless indebtedness we feel to them for all their trouble and concern.

In addition to the specific funerals and memorials celebrated by a family for particular individuals on this increasingly complex calendar, there is the annual observance of Obon, when *all* the deceased members of a family or community are entertained with feasting and dancing. Observed nowadays in August, the Obon, or Urabon Festival, was originally celebrated on the fifteenth of July on the older lunar calendar. On the first day of the festival, according to Japanese belief, the souls of the dead come back to visit their homes and families for two or three days.

Although practically everyone celebrates Obon to some extent, those families who have lost someone during the current year are especially involved in the preparations and festivities. On the first evening of the festival, a small fire is lit in the yard to light the way for the souls on their way home. People without a yard will light a candle, or perhaps some wood chips by the front door of the house; in some places, fires are ignited on nearby mountains. In older times, people lit torches or lanterns all the way from the cemetery or the nearby mountains (where spirits are also thought to dwell) to their homes.

An altar in the home is decorated with various offerings of food and flowers, as well as straw figures of horses and cattle, to honor not only the family's dead souls, but those of others who no longer have relatives in the vicinity. Offerings are placed before the tablets with ancestors' names which stand on the family altar. Sutras may be read and

Ghost appearing in a snowstorm. Artist and date unknown.

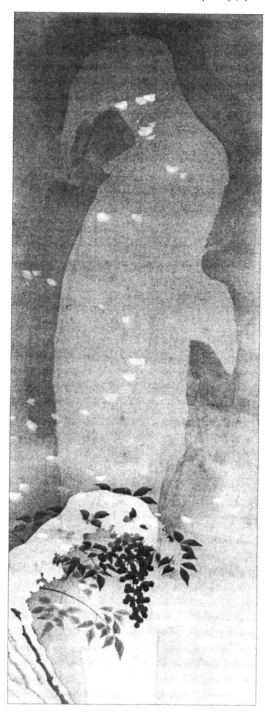

other prayers offered. In many communities, a particular dance is performed, usually with everyone joining in. The *bon-odori*, performed during evening hours, is a dance which has developed from (or in conjunction with) the medieval *nenbutsu-odori* (literally, Buddha-invocation dance), and each locale has developed its own particular set of tunes and distinctive dance steps.

On the third day of Obon, the families send their spirit relations back to the "other side" with farewell fires, often in the form of small lanterns which are allowed to float down a river or away on an outgoing tide. The fires are believed to accompany the souls back to the world of the dead and oblige them to go.

Before the advent of Buddhism in Japan, there already was a custom of inviting the spirits of ancestors back to their homes twice a year, spring and fall, always in connection with a full moon; thus the basic custom possesses the character of an ancestor-veneration festival, which has much in common with the New Year's observance. According to Buddhist beliefs, the Ura-Bon-Sutra (Sanskrit, *ullam-bana*) concerns the legend of Moku-ren, a student of Buddha, who wanted to rescue his mother from the world hunger devil, Gakido. Buddha instructed him to have all the monks make hundreds of food offerings; by so doing, he would be able to lighten the pains of seven generations. For Japanese Buddhists, the legend, of course, has functioned as a lesson in filial piety, as well as suggesting the indigenous relationships among family, ancestors, and food.

As an official celebration combining all these elements, Urabon was apparently practiced for the first time during the fourteenth year of the reign of Empress Suiko (A.D. 606); by 733, the festival had become a customary, courtly Buddhist holiday in Japan. Nonetheless, Yanagita has pointed out that its pre-Buddhist origins are suggested by the fact that *bon* is an earlier term for a plate for offerings to the ancestors; he felt that later Buddhist theologians, and the people themselves, had rationalized the two systems into one. Although the derivation of the term *bon* remains unresolved among scholars, it is intriguing to note that the pre-Buddhist religion of Tibet was called *bon*, suggesting—if the term is not a wild coincidence—an ancient and widespread origin for some of these concepts.

Konno Ensuke, a Japanese folklorist, gives numerous examples of contemporary legends illustrating these values and using these motifs; their content, mood, and logic are very similar to the somewhat older legends in our collection, and eloquently testify to the continuity of traditional stories into the present day. In one very well-known legend, a Tokyo taxi driver picks up a young woman in front of a hospital late one night. She asks to be driven to Hamachō, and when he inquires further about the address, she gives detailed directions. When the driver approaches the right neighborhood, however, he looks into the mirror and sees that she is not there anymore. He thinks perhaps she has fallen asleep or become ill and slumped down in the seat, so he stops at a traffic signal and turns around to find that she has vanished. He feels the seat and finds it terribly cold (a sign that a ghost has been there).

The light has changed, and the other drivers behind him start to blow their horns, so he drives on. Soon he hears her voice again, and she now asks to be driven to Aoyama. Later she asks to be taken back to Hamachō, and when he arrives at the desired address, he can smell incense from a funeral, but she makes no further sound or appearance. The driver stops people who are leaving the house and describes what has happened to him. They explain to him that a young woman of their family died the previous day in that hospital, and that they have just finished the first part of her funeral. The family pays the taxi driver for his trouble, but he is still puzzled, for he wonders why the young woman wanted to go to Aoyama. They conclude that she had a lover in that neighborhood and felt the need to visit him and say farewell.

Konno notes that the incident supposedly happened in 1950, and was reported in the *Yomiuri Shimbun* by a writer, Ishihara Shintaro, whose friend had ridden in the taxi shortly afterward and heard the story directly from the driver. The folklorist immediately recognizes this narrative as a classic example of the "vanishing hitchhiker" legend written about at length by Jan Harold Brunvand, and notes the attribution of the story to "a friend of a friend," the method of proof so common in legends. But such observations would not lessen the impact of this legend upon the Japanese audience, who hear in it a number of motifs which are so common that they "ring true" to cultural values and expectations.

In fact, when we recently asked a Tokyo cabdriver whether he had carried any ghostly passengers, he answered with relief that he had not, but had heard from several of his colleagues about their unsettling adventures with disappearing passengers. "If you're really interested in ghosts," he volunteered, "there's a temple near here that's absolutely full of them!" Some scouting in the area led us eventually to Zenshōan, which indeed owns a collection of some fifty portraits of ghosts which may be viewed by the public only during August, the Obon season.

Other contemporary legends mentioned by Konno include a phantom car which drives around without a visible driver, ghosts seen on airplanes, ghosts of accidentally killed people appearing at railroad crossings in the years right after trains went into service, stories about haunted houses, accounts of deceased persons (especially soldiers during wartime) appearing to their families to bid farewell, ghosts solving mysteries for police (by indicating the location of a hidden grave, for example), children's sighting of ghosts which cannot be seen by adults, and out-of-body experiences described as dreams and omens.

According to one story, ostensibly reported in the newspapers at the time, a Shinjuku-Enoshima express train (one of the privately owned rail lines) struck and killed two sisters at a railroad crossing in 1940. Twelve years later, a third sister was killed on the same spot. After that time in 1952, the ghosts of the three sisters appeared regularly to the engineer on particularly dark nights. The family demanded that more safety devices be erected and also called upon the company to place a proper memorial on the spot. Since these measures were carried out in 1961, no more sightings have been reported.

In the 1950s, a newly trained and graduated stewardess, Miss Morita, was on her first trip from Tokyo to Hong Kong. As she finished her work, she felt someone had called her name, and began to experience a strange sensation. She looked out the plane window and saw a pale woman's face outside; then she heard the woman call her. The woman wore a kimono, had shoulder-length hair, and looked soaking wet. Morita thought at first that she had seen her own face reflected, but then she recognized it belonged to a former colleague, Takagawa Tomoko, who had been murdered in Tokyo. She had been planning to be on this same flight. Later, in the Hong Kong airport as the passengers deplaned, a European woman came up to Morita and asked her where the other stewardess was, the one who had come out of the stewardess's compartment during the flight to help her with something. But Morita had been the only stewardess on board.

Konno notes that legends such as these are being told in Japan by people of all ages and in every walk of life: poets and prominent people as well as professionals, workers, and country folk. Yanagita would conclude, surely, that the Japanese have brought their traditions with them into the present.

In any case, legends—whether ancient, Meiji era, postwar, or contemporary—give us actual texts we can deal with and respond to. More problematic for non-Japanese people are the many customs in contemporary Japan which are important to the Japanese because they are *not* practiced: taboos, which are observed by avoiding dangerous actions altogether. Since the outsider never (or seldom) sees these actions, they tend to remain unclassified, unarticulated, invisible. Thus it is that even the visitor who pays close attention to the cultural signals he *can* see and decode may remain unaware that his bed has been placed so that his head will not be toward the north. He will seldom, if ever, see chopsticks standing upright in a bowl of rice, and will very likely never see people passing food from one pair of chopsticks to another. He may never notice that his sushi has three or five or seven different colors in the middle, but never four (if he does notice it, he will probably attribute it to the Japanese preference for odd numbers in designs).

He will virtually never see these things, unless a child (or he himself) makes a mistake and is quickly corrected, or unless he gets invited to a funeral and suddenly sees all these in action, along with others. These matters are extremely important, for—unlike overt legends or rituals—they form the silent, understood matrix of everyday assumptions. This is information which any visitor needs desperately to know but will seldom hear; more importantly, these beliefs underlie the gestures we see in the legends and in prints, plays, films, and literature. If legends are the "literature" of cultural values, then these customs are the "dance" of culture. And the language in which both are expressed carries a tremendous symbolic load.

At the typical Buddhist funeral, the corpse normally lies with its head to the north, on the *kita makura*, "north pillow," a position considered therefore extremely unlucky for the living. Nearby, on the altar, stands a bowl with one (*ippon bashi*) or two chopsticks standing upright in the rice. In earlier times, this was probably a signal to the deceased that he or she was now eating the "food of the other side," *yomotsu hegui*, and was no longer a part of the circle of living persons. The rice is often called *makura meshi*, "pillow rice," because of its position next to the pillow of the departed, ready for use as a lunch on the way to *anoyo*. The actual method of cooking and preparing the rice varies, of course, by region. The customary *ippon bashi* is a signal that the food is not to be shared with the living.

In the *Kojiki*, initiation into society was often signified by sharing the same vessels; since one wants to *avoid* the society of the dead, various visual and symbolic means are employed to sharpen the distinction between utensils and food used by the living and by the dead, even while the ritual deepens the relationships between the two. While the spirit of the departed person is served in this symbolic way, the living at the funeral ceremony are fed different, but equally meaningful, items, most often in the form of sushi with four colored ingredients in the center; the phoneme for four, *shi*, also means "death," and such food is considered appropriate only for a funeral.

When the body is prepared for the funeral, it is bathed with "reverse water," *sakasa mizu*, where hot water is added to cold, in contrast to the normal way of preparing a bath for the living, where hot water is cooled (if desired) by the addition of cold. The body is then dressed in a kimono which is folded opposite to the normal fashion, that is, *hidarimae*, right over left (the way women's shirts are buttoned in Western cultures). Needless to say, these procedures are considered inappropriate for living persons because per se they suggest preparation for a funeral.

Most Japanese avoid wearing shoes or *zōri* while inside a house because of the *tatami* on the floor. Of course, on practical grounds it is cleaner for the house and kinder to the woven straw mats; but this custom also has to do with funerals, where only the corpse wears shoes or sandals, along with the bearers who carry the coffin out of the house at the conclusion of the ceremony. Numerical aspects of gift giving are also affected: normally one avoids giving things in even numbers, but in addition, one never offers anyone only one cup of tea to drink or one bowl of rice to eat or a single flower, for these practices are associated with funerals and may not be a part of everyday behavior.

These avoidances suggest the sense of sympathetic magic: an action, however symbolic, may actually bring about the reality it represents. Thus, using clothes, foods, or utensils in a manner reserved for funerals may actually precipitate a funeral; people who act inappropriately thus dramatize their own omens of death. In all respects, the behavior of the living is supposed to be clearly distinguished from that of the dead.

Actions, clearly, are powerful, but the same is true for words and phrases; one does not serve someone else three slices of anything because *mikire*, "three slices," also means "to cut the body." One should never write three pages of anything, or four pages (*shimai*, which also means "final end"). One never refers to a single slice of food, for *hito kire* also means "to stab someone." Departing on a trip on the seventh day (*nanoka tabidachi*) is unlucky since it suggests the seventh-day funeral observance. Because the words for *four* and *nine* (*shi, ku*) also are homophones for death (*shi*) and torture, agony, suffering (*ku*), people in many parts of Japan avoid uttering the phonemes for these numbers in contexts where the meaning seems ambiguous.

It is important to remember that these ambiguities exist in conversation and not in writing, because the characters for these words are indeed quite different. Thus, the word for "comb," *kushi*, when written, does not contain the characters for death and suffering but, when spoken, its sound triggers complicated cultural associations which are not part of the literal meaning.

Associations surrounding the comb (*kushi*) are numerous and rich, and are illustrated in several of the legends in this collection. Combs seem to take on the personality or spirit of their owners and so their appearance in connection with a ghost is more than a matter of fashion or decoration. Further, in combination with deeply held ideas about the importance of hair and hairstyle, the comb suggests imagery which cannot be grasped easily by outsiders. Consider: *kami*, used in reference to the hair of the head (more fully, *kami no ke*, "uppermost hair") echoes the word *kami* (local god) because it is also uppermost; *kushi* (comb) sounds like the older term for hair (*ogushi* or *migushi*, the prefixes functioning as honorifics); *ku* and *shi*, as noted, refer homophonically to death and agony. Put all these together orally (or visually in a picture of a ghost, for example), and the result is a reverberating cluster of implications more than adequate to infuse a narrative with an emotionally charged load of cultural meaning.

Other associations with numbers lie more in custom than homophony, but they still exist in the fact that they govern everyday behavior. For example, in Nagasaki Prefecture, it is considered a taboo for two people to clean the house at the same time; in Ōita, two people should not place things into the same container at the same time; in many parts of Japan, it is considered taboo for both parents to put shoes on the same child simultaneously; in Hokkaidō, two people should not sweep the same room together; in several areas, two people should not wash their feet in the same tub together. The origins of such taboos are not clear, but since they are reminiscent of funeral practices (for example, usually two people remove the bones after a cremation and put them in one container), we can deduce that the avoidance is based—as in the cases mentioned earlier—on the feeling that language and actions related to the dead must be strictly separated from the everyday business of living.

This is not to say that every Japanese person today avoids these expressions and actions because of an immediate fear of death, for many of these "taboos" have become so common that they function chiefly as indications of polite behavior—just as many Americans say, "Bless you!" after someone sneezes without necessarily believing that the soul of the sneezer was in danger of being snatched by the devil. Nonetheless, most Japanese can explain why such customs are maintained, and children who start to pass food from one set of chopsticks to another will be quickly scolded with the comment that such behavior belongs only at cremations. Similarly, because the postcremation chopsticks for passing fragments of bone are intentionally mismatched (for example, one of wood, one of bamboo), using two different kinds of *hashi* to eat with is abhorrent, and parents will immediately correct a child who has inadvertently chosen an unmatched pair. Parents may or may not be able to explain why children who trim their nails after dark are destined not to reach their parents' deathbed in time, but the survival of the saying surely indicates that the filial obligation to be at that deathbed continues to be stressed (not following this maxim's advice suggests that one doesn't care about one's parents).

Whether these avoidance patterns are maintained today by some people for the sake of politeness, or whether they still carry a heavy freight of meaning is probably impossible to assess accurately, for in actuality there is a great range of personal involvement with these cultural codes. Nonetheless, their persistence, along with a consistent use of ghost and death imagery in contemporary legend, literature, and film, does indicate a cultural richness which, if appreciated, might make us more aware of that "other side of the stairway" discussed in Part I.

For one thing, it may come as a surprise to the occidental reader brought up on those grim stereotypical accounts of hara-kiri and kamikaze attacks in World War II that in Japanese culture, there is a stress on the seriousness of death and the responsibilities connected with it, accompanied by an extremely delicate avoidance of actions and words suggesting death. Have we not read that life is cheap in Asia, that the individual counts for little, and that suicide is a common expression of Asian disregard for human existence?

Joseph Campbell, writing in *The Masks of God: Oriental Mythology*, claims that regard for life on one hand, and disregard of death on the other, provide a cultural "watershed" that distinguishes Western from Eastern myth and culture. In his view, the apparent lack of deep concern over the deaths of individuals in the Orient (reflected in part by suttee in India and a high suicide rate in Japan) grows naturally from religions which have depicted the individual as relatively unimportant in comparison to the larger issues of nature and morality. Western religions, in contrast, concentrate more on the individual, keeping close watch over personal achievements and sins, and thus encourage the idea that the life of every person is sacred and worthy of maintenance.

Like many of Campbell's generalizations, this one sounds reasonable enough until we encounter the mixed evidence offered by everyday life and expression; for quite unlike the elite myths which dramatize the concerns of religious leaders (often phrased in moving, but monolithic, terms), the "texts" and details of everyday life exhibit the pulse of what people are actually feeling. And these texts, whatever form they may take, are best decoded according to their contexts and not by superficial comparisons with apparently similar or diverse topics made by observers.

For example, it is possible to argue that suttee in India, far from being a barbarous practice exercised by a culture which considered life cheap, was a sacrificial action dramatizing exactly the opposite: that life is the most precious thing one can give. As another instance, we now recognize that suicide is probably as common in the United States as Japan (some have suggested the northern European rate is even higher); will this lead us then to argue that the West now pays *less* attention to the individual than it once did?

Japanese legends, literature, and film indicate that life may be viewed as so special that a murder can be even more abhorrent, more poignant, and more laced with guilt than it ever could in the West. And a Japanese suicide—far from being an expression of worthlessness or bleak despair (though it may be these as well)—can be seen as braver, more ironic, or more aggressive than it would be for a Western person. Campbell was correct in his insistence that attitudes toward death are culture centered, but perhaps his Western bias helped him overlook the complexity and delicacy of meaning in situations where surface similarities or contrasts may imply massively different assumptions and meanings.

The Japanese are surrounded by death imagery and taboo (whether deeply or superficially perceived) on just about every level of everyday life. If it is a question of "when the living let go of the dead," it is the Western world which seems rather strongly disposed to have the funeral and get on with life, thus in a way reducing the importance of the deceased. A single funeral is held, or perhaps in the case of some Catholics a series of masses (subscribed to by the family but performed by proxy without the necessity of family presence), a notice is placed in the paper, and then the relatives go on with their lives and let the dead rest in peace. The Japanese, by comparison, do not let go. Their ritual, their behavior, their legends, their taboos remind them constantly of those enduring mutual obligations to family, clan, and nation. And their dead do not rest: they are busy helping the family.

Ruth Benedict and others have commented fully on these matters, but even the foremost scholars have tended to refer to historical documents and formal sources for their examples; and their discussion has been mostly in the language of intellectual history and philosophy, and not in the expressive genres of everyday oral tradition. This more widespread, more common dimension is a powerful one because it engages people's emotions, loyalties, passions, experiences, and guilt better than it reflects their conscious philosophies, a fact which modern filmmakers have grasped more quickly than others. Films like Nakagawa Nobuo's *The Living Koheiji*,

A ghost who yearns for candlelight. Artist: Tani Bun'itsu (1786–1818). Born the son of a doctor in the part of Edo (now Tokyo) called Nihonbashi, the artist was later adopted by the painter Tani Bunkō.

Shindō Kaneto's *Onibaba* and *Kuroneko*, Kinoshita Keisuke's *Yotsuya Kaidan*, Mori Kazuo's *The Ghost of Oiwa*, Kobayashi Masaki's *Kwaidan*, and Mizoguchi Kenji's *Ugetsu Monogatari* not only testify to the fact that death and ghosts are still viable subject matters in Japanese popular films, but since these films are recognized as being among the finest of Japanese filmmakers' art, they indicate the depth of creative possibility available to serious artists who avail themselves of their culture's riches.

The evocative power seems to rest, as it does in the orally transmitted legends, in the ambiguity of interwoven worlds; there is little or no demarcation between the worlds of the living and the dead, family obligations do not cease with death, living humans may meet ghosts anytime, and people may see visions which only later are understood to have a meaning. The fields of illusion and reality overlap and interact, and may indeed not be distinguishable, and this allows for the kind of ambiguity and simultaneity which can thrive on anxiety and guilt, which can produce delicious ironies, and which can create the most stunning of tragedies.

Moreover, in the actions of an angry ghost, feelings of guilt, selfishness, jealousy, and betrayal can be acted out in metaphorical tableau scenes which would be repressed in everyday life. That is, human emotions which do indeed exist and animate much of the culture can be dramatized and perceived vicariously through a ghost character who represents in physical form the otherwise abstract and possibly embarrassing emotion which would normally be too volatile to express in personal interaction.

The repressed guilts, anxieties, and debts—along with their emotional expressions of anger and frustration—can also be released in laughter; an excellent example is the 1984 film *The Funeral*, directed by Itami Jūzō, in which the oppressive obligations of a funeral are so fully and ridiculously portrayed that Japanese audiences usually collapse in laughter.

Like Kabuki and Nō plays, the legend narratives dramatize in very intensely focused fashion a stressful moment in which individual desire is juxtaposed to social or cultural demand: the passions of a particular individual (a strong desire to see a loved one, to be beautiful, to get land, to travel somewhere, to catch a lot of fish) are played off against the cultural need for harmony, ritual, order, cooperation, and conformity. In Japanese legends, it is usually the community value which triumphs in the end: a ghost is pacified and the village can rest; a child is ritualized into the community and becomes a monk who serves the religious needs of the area; sisters killed by a train are memorialized, and their ghosts no longer haunt the engineer.

In contrast, when the proper order is not achieved, the area and all those who live there or pass through it remain subject to the anxieties of the unresolved problem; so to speak, they are haunted by unfinished business—hearing strange noises in the mountains, seeing flames in the cemetery, feeling hunger in remote places, seeing a child's sad face in the house rafters or the heads of drowned fishermen floating on the waters. It would be difficult to imagine a more effective system of reminding people of their unresolved debts and obligations and thus of the necessity of keeping dramatically alive the emotional foundations of a culture through recurrent narrative experiences. Japanese legends are powerful and enduring because they are a concrete articulation of important and deep abstract values; like poetry, they make feelings and ideas palpable.

Suggested Reading and Related Resources

A solid account of modern storytellers is given by V. Hrdličková in "Japanese Professional Storytellers," in *Folklore Genres*, edited by Dan Ben-Amos (Austin: University of Texas Press, 1976), 171–90. Some modern short stories, many of them focusing on death, appear in the fine collection *The Mother of Dreams and Other Short Stories: Portrayals of Women in Modern Japanese Fiction*, edited by Ueda Makoto (Tokyo, New York, San Francisco: Kōdansha International, 1986); Kawabata's "Tabi" is on pp. 24–26, and his "Fushi" on pp. 27–29; Abe's "Shinda musume ga utatta..." appears on pp. 227–39; Hiraiwa's "Yūgao no onna" is on pp. 259–77. Fosco Maraini's *Japan: Patterns of Continuity* (Tokyo and New York: Kōdansha International, 1971) is richly illustrated with striking photographs, which show (sometimes through the creative use of coincidence) similarities between art and nature, old and new, ritual and everyday.

Ichirō Hori discusses *goryō* and the *nembutsu* response to it in his *Folk Religion in Japan: Continuity and Change* (Chicago: University of Chicago Press, 1968), 111–27. The various terms for aspects of the soul and parts of the funeral observances are covered by Hori in the same work; as well, see Matsudaira Narimitsu, "The Concept of

Tamashii in Japan," in *Studies in Japanese Folklore*, edited by Richard Dorson (Bloomington: Indiana University Press, 1963), 181–97; also the reader with facility in Japanese is urged to consult Yanagita Kunio's *Sōsō shūzoku goi* (Folk vocabulary concerning funeral and memorial rites and ceremonies) (Tokyo: Iwanami-shoten, 1937).

Ruth Benedict's description of the Japanese culture is one of the fullest ever produced by a non-Japanese. Her discussion of *on* and related obligations, debts, and "repayments" covers four chapters: "Debtor to the Ages and the World," "Repaying One-Ten-Thousandth," "The Repayment 'Hardest to Bear'," and "Clearing One's Name," in *The Chrysanthemum and the Sword: Patterns of Japanese Culture* (Boston: Houghton Mifflin, 1946), 98–176. The very bulk of her treatment is an indication of *on*'s import to an understanding of the whole culture.

Some Japanese sources for details on the traditions of funerals are Koike Nagayuki, *Hito no shigo no hanashi* (Tokyo: Gakugei Tosho, 1970); Ōtsuka-Minzoku-Gakkai, *Nihon Minzoku-jiten* (Tokyo: Kōbundō, 1971); *Nihon Kokugo Daijiten*, 6th ed. (Tokyo: Shōgakukan, 1986); Watanabe Shōkō, *Shigo no sekai* (Tokyo: Iwanami-shoten, 1959).

Accounts of funerals in rural villages, based on contemporary observation, are provided by Robert J. Smith in "The Life Cycle," in *Japanese Character and Culture*, edited by Bernard S. Silberman (Tucson: University of Arizona Press, 1962), 206, 213; and in Richard K. Beardsley, John W. Hall and Robert E. Ward, *Village Japan* (Chicago: University of Chicago Press, 1959), 338–43.

The heavy use of sevens and multiples of seven, according to Inokuchi Shōji, may derive from the subdivision of the lunar month, which provides a system for rituals involving death and childbirth: an essentially twenty-eight-day cycle is divided into four parts, two coming before the full moon and two afterward. These seven-day units seem to have become the means of measuring ritually important activity: for the first seven days after a death, for example, the family members are considered impure, and each succeeding unit of seven days—until the forty-ninth day—implements the process of purification. On the forty-ninth day, the family is freed from the strict abstinences associated with the funeral. Twenty-one days after birth, a baby is brought to a Shintō shrine by its mother. Preparations for religious rituals are similarly divided into seven-day segments betokening the units of purification or abstinence associated with the particular rite. Inokuchi suggests that this seven-day system, found prominently throughout Asia, might have been the origin of the seven-day-week concept in the west (*Nihon no Zokushin* [Tokyo: Kōbundō,

1975], 53–76).

Hori points out that while some families may honor the fiftieth or the hundredth anniversary of a death for symbolic purposes, the spirit of the dead person is believed to retain its identity only until the thirty-third anniversary (*tomuraiage,* "completion of the personal memorial service"), at which point the person has become one with the ancestral *kami.* Unfortunately, Hori's important works are not widely available in English; his informative *Folk Religion in Japan,* already cited, is an excellent example of his command of vernacular belief and expression. A number of related insights can be found in his essay, "The Appearance of Individual Self-Consciousness in Japanese Religion and Its Historical Transformations," in *The Japanese Mind: Essentials of Japanese Philosophy and Culture,* edited by Charles A. Moore (Honolulu: University of Hawaii Press, 1967), 201–27. Kishimoto Hideo's remarks on death being a part of Japanese life are found in his essay, "Some Japanese Cultural Traits and Religions," on pp. 118–20 of the same work.

The double grave and its historical connections are discussed by Mogami Takayoshi in "The Double Grave System," in Dorson's *Studies in Japanese Folklore,* 167–80; on pp. 181–97 in the same collection, the essay by Matsudaira entitled "Tamashii" includes a number of details about funeral customs, taboos, and nuances, including the inevitable comment on chopsticks sticking upright in the rice bowl. As well, Sunada Toshiko, in her informative pamphlet on Japanese food traditions, *Japanese Food and Good Old Wisdom* (Tokyo: Ajinomoto Co., 1985), takes care to observe that chopsticks are never to be used in a way that can connote death or constitute a bad omen (19). Yanagita's comments on Obon appear in *Senzo no hanashi* (About our ancestors), vol. 10 of his collected works, *Teihon Yanagita Kunio-shū* (Tokyo: Chikuma-shobō, 1985) 78–84. See also Hori's comments on Obon in *Folk Religion in Japan* on pp. 138–39 and 156–60.

Among Americans, a favorite book about everyday Japanese culture is the three-volume compendium produced by various writers for the Yamaguchi family, proprietors of the Fujiya Hotel; entitled *We Japanese,* it gives numerous brief examples of Japanese customs, festivals, ceremonies, and manners for the instruction and edification of travelers to Japan (Miyanoshita, Japan: Fujiya Hotel, various dates). The book provides a whole page of common customs and taboos related to death, supplying visitors to the country with information on proper etiquette (which is, no doubt, a benefit for visitor and native alike).

The contemporary legends mentioned in this chapter are among the many recounted by Konno Ensuke in *Nihon kaidan-shū:*

Yūrei-hen (Collected Japanese sinister stories: human specters) (Tokyo: Shakaishisōsha, Ltd., 1969).

Characters and motifs from ghost legends have been among the most popular subjects for painters and printmakers. On page 204 of James Michener's *The Hokusai Sketch-Books*, (Tokyo and Rutland, Vt.: Tuttle, 1958), there is a print of Kasane, an incredibly ugly young woman who inherits a plot of land from her mother. A peasant, Yoemon, marries Kasane in order to get the land, then murders her. Her ghost haunts the area until a monk, Yūten, exorcises her. Yūten later becomes a bishop, Yoemon a monk. Michener also has a print of *The Ghost of Kiku and the Priest Mikazuki* on page 205, an illustration of the legend and Kabuki play about the girl who is accused of breaking one of ten porcelain plates. In the convention of depicting ghosts, Kiku is shown with no feet. The catalog for a 1985–86 art exhibition sponsored by the Spencer Museum of Art (University of Kansas) provides a splendid array of examples: *Japanese Ghosts and Demons: Art of the Supernatural*, edited by Stephen Addiss (New York: George Braziller, 1985) displays hundreds of ghosts, among them Kohada Koheiji (the ghost of a betrayed husband; see color plate), Oyuki (the ghost of a young mistress), Okiku (accused of breaking the precious plate), Oiwa (the disfigured victim of her husband's greed), along with the weeping rock, and sundry demons, goblins, walking skeletons, foxes, toads and monsters.

Joseph Campbell's monumental four-volume work, *The Masks of God* (New York: Viking Press, 1959–68) raises as many questions as it answers; nonetheless, the second volume (1962) provides a sweeping view of the basic religious systems of India, China, Japan, and Tibet and brings many trends and processes into focus. On pp. 475–76, he reports a conversation between a western sociologist and a Shintō priest in which the latter insists that there is no articulated ideology or theology in Shintō: "We do not have a theology," the priest says; "we dance," thus emphasizing that it is personal involvement with nature which is important—the sense, as Campbell puts it, of "living in gratitude and awe amid the mystery of things" (477). Impressive as the comment is, it of course artfully overlooks the extensive theology of Shintō.

The films mentioned in this chapter remain popular in Japan, as well as in American film festivals and art-film series. Most of them were included in the University of California at Berkeley's Pacific Film Archive series in 1986, and many appear regularly on cable television in California, where the great number of Japanese and Japanese American viewers keep them in demand.

Part III

Japanese Death Legends and Vernacular Culture

The legends in this collection are but one genre of the many which make up the traditional expressions of Japanese folklife. Because legends include archaic cultural ideas, antiquarians find in them a record of outmoded, vanished, or "primitive" concepts which have been left behind by the culture as it approached its modern form. To teachers and library storytellers, legends seem to provide relatively safe examples of childish mentality, naive experience, and uncomplicated science. Because of their anonymity and constant variation, legends strike some historians as interesting, quaint, but certainly unreliable accounts with little factual basis to recommend them as subjects for study.

To folklorists and social historians, however, a legend represents an articulate dramatization of cultural meaning—quite regardless of the extent to which it contains "factual" information. In a legend, an intense tableau scene is capable of triggering in the audience a rich and complex set of deeply shared cultural values. Just as the story of "The Three Little Pigs" is not *about* pigs, but uses them to say something about humans who try to keep the wolf from the door, so the legend of Oiwa is not simply *about* a disfigured female ghost but rather a dramatization of Japanese attitudes on marital obligations, betrayal of family, and selfishness, as well as an enactment of otherwise abstract ideas about spirits and their emotional condition. Legends may be interesting to children, but they are seldom just "kid stuff," for they are threads in the fabric of meaning which animates a whole culture. Moreover, the elements of anonymity and variation which bother the scholar looking only for facts and "reliable" data are the very characteristics which mark all folklore as having been refined by a considerable number of people in its development.

The importance of this? Unlike a book, which continues to exist long after its composition whether anyone reads it or not, folk traditions endure only because people share them in daily interactions. If a folk tradition—such as a legend—has persisted over the years, it is only because a considerable number of people have found it worth repeating to each other; otherwise it would have died out. Thus we can reasonably assume that the legend has continued to "mean" something or play some important role for those who perform it. Armed with that assumption, we can ask what this meaning might be, even if we never obtain a final, exact answer.

Folktales, legends, beliefs, and the like probably persist because as they develop, they bring together a recognizable constellation of related beliefs and cultural traditions phrased in vivid, concrete detail (much like a fine poem). As Jan Harold Brunvand has noted, narrative performances of American contemporary legends are extremely accurate reflections of popular prejudices and assumptions about how things happen in an unpredictable world, and do not seem influenced by "objective" logic. The community appears to feel more at ease with an internal logic which verifies existing values rather than holding them up to objective (outside) scrutiny.

Because the esoteric groups in which all forms of folklore flourish may be as large as nations or as small as families, folklorists have defined their field of inquiry more by the genres themselves than the varied groups. To be sure, more recent studies have focused on the folklore of groups: familial, occupational, ethnic, religious, regional. But over the years, folklorists have commented mostly on particular kinds of folklore: custom, belief, vernacular architecture, folk foods, regional dialect, traditional crafts, folk songs (lullabies, work songs, etc.), tales (Märchen, jokes), rhymes, charms, gestures, games, and legends. A list of this sort of course tells us something, but it does not indicate why all these apparently disparate genres should or can be grouped under the same rubric: "folklore." Actually, however, their common denominator is not difficult to find: it is their common and ongoing vernacular currency among closely associated people.

The vernacular tradition, in contrast to the formal, learned channels in any society, is based on everyday associations and expressions; social interaction is usually oral, aural, and gestural; "performances"—whether the telling of a joke, the building of a fence, the making of a quilt or a *zabuton*, the relating of a legend—are done for close associates in familiar settings and circumstances. Because the material is "live" instead of set in print, it tends to vary with each articulation, so that in the long run, the culturally acceptable idea or design survives, not a single, particularized "original."

Vernacular expressions performed in recurring, culturally important situations: this is what the folklorist seeks. Since vernacular expressions exist only as long as people perform them for each other, a more satisfying question than "What is folklore?" or "What is folk legend?" is the more complex query, "Why, by whom, and for what reasons do people keep telling legends?" If this question can only be answered with the observation that people are simply gullible and illogical, then, of course, a book like this is hardly worth bothering with. On the other hand, if the same themes, anxieties, concerns, and values found in a group of legends are also prominently displayed in the daily lives of the people who tell them, then we have another perspective to deal with; for whether we agree with their logic or not, we may find that these legends offer one of the best possibilities for insight into an ongoing culture. When the culture under discussion is as large and influential as Japan's is in the modern world, and when we realize how little other cultures know about the feel and style of everyday Japanese life (in spite of all the avuncular handbooks on how to do business like a samurai), then a seemingly quaint subject like ghost stories constitutes a richer resource than first expected.

Where does one find such traditions, and how does the interested person bring the material into an accurate enough focus that it can be understood and appreciated without the inevitable distortions wrought by outside scrutiny? We are fortunate to have the field researches of many avid Japanese folklorists from the turn of this century to the present. The legends included here as separate texts are given as closely as possible to the ways in which the collectors took them down from the narrations of their informants—who were often their neighbors, family members, friends. Many of the legends are still being told in Japan as well as other communities in Brazil, Canada, and the United States where Japanese people have settled. Even where a particular type of legend has died out, the premises on which ghost legends are based still provide a strong, ongoing constellation of meaning for contemporary Japanese. Everyday anecdotes, gestures, and assumptions may seem insignificant when perceived separately, but in the aggregate, when seen in a film or Kabuki play or novel, they convey strong emotional meaning for the insider (and serious puzzlement for the outsider)—clearly not a negligible matter after all.

The materials normally examined in folklore studies arise from, and persist in, everyday traditional situations among closely associated persons. There may naturally be an overlap or a borrowing between the vernacular and the classical, such as when a Kabuki play is based on a traditional legend; nonetheless, folklorists look at the everyday cultural meaning of the story and not at the formal training or individual creativity of a classical artist. Of course, in this approach there can be no certainty that the story will "mean" exactly the same thing for all tellers and listeners; nor is there an assumption that all members of a culture will respond in the same way. Nonetheless, when we notice that certain themes and topics continually appear in similar constellations of situation and meaning, it would be foolish to overlook the possibility of cultural sharing. It is not unreasonable to believe that a person raised in a "high context" culture—where information is normally exchanged without technical explanation and certain stories and topics recur in similar patterns—has grown up with a working understanding of a culturally acceptable range of meanings derived from the hearing (and perhaps telling) of many texts. A person growing up in the United States can hardly avoid knowing what will follow from the introductory line "There was this traveling salesman, and. . . ."

*A woman's ghost.
The image is rare
because Japanese
ghosts usually are
depicted without
feet. Artist: Satake
Eiko (1834–1909).*

This phenomenon might be called "intertextuality" by some, but in fact it is the shared ideas and their connotations that interact and inform each other; the texts are only the media in which the ideas achieve dramatic form. For these reasons, the folkloristic approach today assumes a combined attitude toward these vernacular expressions, whatever form they may take; this approach can be described as a happy marriage of literary analysis, anthropological or ethnological resource work, and historical interpretation.

The literary aspect of folklore simply views any vernacular expression as a "text" with implied cultural meanings. Whether one is talking about a traditionally built house, a regionally distinct food or preparation method, a folk song, or a legend, its articulation is assumed to have community-based meaning, symmetry, structure, nuance, style—all matters which can be perceived and discussed in relation to the particular culture from which it emanates. Instead of dealing with the product of a singular genius, folklorists study the persistent expressions of the relatively anonymous masses as they are passed along through time and space.

There are many differences between written and oral literature, but there is little distinction in analytical perspective: the Hemingway scholar tries to read everything the author wrote—good, bad, mediocre—and come to grips with meaning, art, impact, significance. The student of legend or tale or folk song does the same—usually without knowing an author's name, but still confronting the same issues and problems. The assumption is the same in both cases: the text is susceptible of analysis and discussion.

But there are obvious differences: Hemingway may have left behind a number of letters and notes and conversations—as well as other published works and manuscripts—so that the scholar can make some fairly intelligent guesses about what a particular passage or story might mean, or what its author's intention was. The folklorist seldom has access to the notes or thoughts of a particular originator but must work with the accumulated expressive corpus of a whole culture. In both cases, scholars must guard against reading anything extraneous into the text, yet be ready to acknowledge that much of the sense may be shaped by the audience's responses. Both believe that human expressions have meaning which can be discussed and that a single analytical observation on a text is probably insufficient.

An important distinction between contemporary oral and written tradition, however, is the fact that literature is produced for the eye and the intellect—it can be read in solitude or on a crowded bus full of strangers; it can be reread or savored passage by passage; in some cases, even the way a word is placed on a page and the space around it convey meaning. Oral tradition is aimed at the ears; one not only hears the legend or tale being told, but actually is surrounded by the sound and many other circumstances of performance. At the same time, the narrator, using his or her breath, vocal cords, eyes, and hands, makes a physical commitment to pass on an important cultural tradition.

Because of this personal, live, emotional involvement, Yanagita Kunio encouraged his students and colleagues to see their personal relationship with the performance as an indispensable aspect of meaning. This seemingly subjective stance later earned him an undeserved reputation for being less than scientific, but it marks him today as a pioneer in insisting that, in the case of real ongoing tradition, the researcher cannot obtain empirically valid results from an objective, outside position. Getting a neighbor to tell a legend makes the collector a part of the audience.

The anthropological or ethnographic dimension of folklore study is concerned with the issue of empirical validity. The folklorist, to document and understand a traditional performance fully, needs to collect it while it is occurring in its normal habitat. Usually this entails fieldwork among performers of whatever tradition the folklorist seeks to record and study. Beyond that, the ethnographer wants to lay bare the cultural aspects of meaning in contradistinction to personal idiosyncratic elements introduced by particular tradition bearers. The inquiry is aimed at what might be called horizontal meaning: what does x mean to the y people? What does this legend mean to the Japanese or the people of a particular village? The whole living culture is seen as a context for meaning and a setting for performance.

But the performance must be viewed empirically, not theoretically recreated, if we are to understand that meaning, for folklore is experientially perceived and disseminated. And since performances vary considerably for a number of reasons, a corollary of this kind of analysis is that there seldom if ever exists a single "meaning" for a particular text. Moreover, because a story is never told to a whole culture at once, its immediate performance context is necessarily narrower than its possibility for cultural meaning. It is unfortunate that early folklore collectors—in the West as well as Japan—did not provide us with all the details of live performance.

The historical view—especially the one developed in recent years by the social historians—is less interested in mere date, data, and sequence than in vertical meanings: what has the legend meant to the Japanese through time, how has it affected their views, how has it shaped or articulated the values which have caused or interpreted historically important events? This is the belief that ongoing culture, especially that of the masses rather than the elite, is the matrix from which important historical processes arise and in which they are judged. Common people's persistent cultural experiences—their traditions—are historically meaningful.

In all of this stress on the vernacular, there is, however, no implication that the everyday culture is more important or "pure" than classical or formal culture; in fact, in every known instance, the two interact so richly that a strict line is impossible to draw. Nonetheless, there is a tendency in a literate society to assume that the formal level is more advanced or more polished or more socially acceptable than that which exists primarily in the streets. So the problem is not with the materials but with the potential snobbishness of those who view them.

It is tempting to speculate on how much more we would know about almost any historical period if we were aware of what was being performed among the everyday people. Knowing about George Washington's achievements does not reveal much about why men were willing to camp out in the snow at Valley Forge; we would learn far more about them if we only had a thirty-minute tape recording of the jokes, legends, and rumors they were telling each other around the campfires. Robert Darnton and Leonard Rosenband have increased our sense of prerevolution France astronomically by focusing on what was going on in the customs and amusements of people in the streets and the working trades. Indeed, knowing what the aggregate of people are doing, saying, and meaning is at the very heart of understanding culture; for, as Yanagita Kunio pointed out, culture is made up of those traditions through which we continue to experience and understand our past within our contemporary world. And for Yanagita, "we" is construed as the collection of everyday people who make up the society: the common people, as expressed by the term *minzoku*—those who make up the *vernacular* culture.

Yanagita Kunio (1875–1962) was probably the greatest single force in the establishment of the *minzokugaku* movement in modern times. Although the usual rendering of that term in English is "folklore," a fuller one would be something like "ethnography of the common people in everyday life." Just as the Latin *vernaculus* (home-born slave) gave the English term "vernacular" a pejorative effect, the Japanese term *jōmin* (something like "commoner") once had a negative connotation which should not be part of the modern definition; folklorists may indeed study rural farmers or fishermen, but they also investigate the traditional customs of the urbanite. The stress is on the everyday rather than the elite, the ongoing oral tradition rather than the written formal one; and Yanagita was sure that the continuing, familiar expressions of Japan carried with them the essence of past values which—instead of disappearing and being abandoned—were repeatedly reexpressed, reoriented, reused, rerationalized in the present. Because much of Japan's older culture resided in rural areas, Yanagita's researches often centered there; but it was the essence of tradition, wherever it dwelt, which fascinated him.

Because of his focus on the Japanese-ness of Japan, he became popular with those who objected to the international borrowings of the Meiji Restoration (1867–1912). As Japan moved into the nationalistic intensity of World War II, Yanagita's works seemed even more exciting and "true." But long after the war, his writings remained popular, and during the 1970s he was still an intellectual force, his collected works (in thirty-six volumes) selling over sixty thousand sets. He wrote more than a hundred books, plus an immense amount of poetry (much of which has never been published or translated); and it is indeed rare, according to Professor Yoneyama Toshinao, to find a home library in Japan that does not include at least some of his works. Praised by many as a leading figure in Japan's modern intellectual search for its identity, revered as an author and poet, admired for his subtle resistance to academic and bureaucratic establishments, he is also suspected by some modern scholars as a dogmatic nationalist and has been rejected by some of his academic descendants as an unscientific scholar mostly because he stressed the personal, subjective dimensions of ethnographic work.

As a result, another branch of *minzokugaku*, using a different *kanji* for *-gaku*, has developed in modern Japan. More sociological and anthropological in their training, the new Japanese folklorists have added an objective and analytical dimension to their field of study, an aspect that might be termed "ethnographic" in English. In fact, since the term *minzokugaku* has developed the same opprobrium in common usage as "folklore" in English (nonsense), scholars often identify their area of interest as *bunka* (culture), which carries a more intellectually respectable connotation.

Nonetheless, scholars in other fields have continued to use Yanagita's precepts, and there has been a tendency to view his role more generously in recent years. For example, Karatani Kōjin has reevaluated Yanagita's work from a modern perspective, and has argued that the folklorist was not simply a mouthpiece for Japanese nationalism (nor even nationalistic per se) but that he created as objective and usable an approach as was possible in his day. In fact, counter to the official nationalistic view of the 1920s and 1930s, he openly espoused the position—based on his studies of folklore—that the Japanese and their culture had not appeared spontaneously on the islands, but came originally from Korea and China. Yanagita's feel for folklore, based on his philosophical search for what it was to be human, was accurate, according to Karatani, and his profound faith in the richness of vernacular expression informed both his personal life and his theoretical approach to the study of culture.

Even so, a modern folklorist does indeed find a number of gaps and flaws in Yanagita's fieldwork and theory; for example, he seems to have avoided much of the sexual aspect of tradition, partly by rewriting field-recorded texts to hide sexual or other potentially embarrassing references, thus reducing the immediacy and accuracy of the very vernacular he was trying to champion. While the rewording of oral texts would not be countenanced by folklorists and ethnographers today, this practice is not enough to eclipse Yanagita's positive influence on the understanding of everyday Japanese culture; and since we are convinced that modern Japanese tradition employs and expresses the same values we see in the older legends, Yanagita's perspectives give us insight and food for thought.

Yanagita insisted that what people continue to do and say and believe is as important as the artifacts they leave behind.

The ghost of a mother appears at the bedside of her beloved child. Artist: Kikuchi Yōsai (1788–1878).

While most of his contemporaries engaged in the study of material folklore and folklife, Yanagita was busy collecting stories, legends, gestures, customs, and beliefs. His heavy stress on *minkan denshō* (folk tradition) was based on his conviction that it, rather than the formal written record, reliably conveys and demonstrates cultural continuity. "Visible history"—the written, formal, and usually elite record of the powerful and famous—is so partial and so focused on single personalities that it cannot give an accurate picture of what is happening in the whole culture. Thus he regarded the standard historical method, dependent mostly on written records from this narrow field of human experience, as incomplete and inaccurate from the start.

During the Meiji era, there was a concerted attempt by establishment scholars and political theorists to rewrite the history of Japan using only elite data. Yanagita politely but obstinately countered with oral tradition gleaned from his interviews with common people. Their "invisible history," he insisted, though not couched in the powerful language of the elite, was broader and more consistent in its attention to and expression of the ongoing values of the masses; thus it was a far more accurate depiction of the Japanese culture. Since historians assume the right to choose which events to record and since written records are relatively few in number (many having been destroyed by fire), the chances are slim that "visible history" will be able to answer sufficiently the questions of succeeding generations. How much less can visible history tell us about those villages where daily lives never get placed on paper, no matter how interesting or distinguished they may be? Only the oral tradition of everyday people can adequately record and pass on those values that remain central to the culture.

If the most important threads of history and culture are invisible, then how does one go about discovering or collecting enough material to study, interpret, and analyze? Yanagita was quite explicit: the researcher must talk to the people directly and not rely on written records. Beyond that, one must talk to them on their own turf and let them do the talking, allow them to create the forms embodying the values. And to accomplish this, one must permit the subjective, experiential aspect of culture to emerge: one does not construct an intellectual or sociological questionnaire and try to elicit answers from sample "subjects."

Tada Michitarō, a follower of Yanagita, tells an instructive anecdote about a researcher who wanted to find out about the retention of a certain old custom in northern Japan; learning the local dialect and constructing a proper questionnaire, he interviewed people and asked if they still felt they owed an obligation to local feudal lords. Over 85 percent reported that they owed nothing to their local lord; a small number, slightly more than 5 percent, felt that they did have some debt. The professor went happily back to his university and wrote a report which claimed that the peasants in the area had been able to rid themselves of traditional obligations to their landlords and had thus made the transition from feudal to modern society without apparent difficulty.

Tada justly faults the results by pointing out two flaws which could have been avoided if the researcher had used Yanagita's approach. First, it should have occurred to anyone—particularly another Japanese—that the farmers would not have admitted to an outsider that they considered themselves anyone's servants or vassals. Second, the researcher should have stayed around long enough to *observe* empirically that most of the farmers in this area do indeed make annual gifts to their landlords and are thus still acting out feudal relationships, even though intellectually they may not describe things that way.

Yanagita's prescriptions for fieldwork are so simple and sensible that it is a wonder they have not attracted more attention worldwide: the study of everyday life requires us to look analytically at those shared expressions which can be (*a*) seen, (*b*) heard, and (*c*) believed. To elaborate, these dimensions or levels of ethnography are as follows:

(*a*) Those things which can be *seen* as traditional items and expressions of everyday life: material culture, gesture, folk art, ritual, dance, festival, custom. These are actions or products which can be observed, noted, sketched, photographed, and described by a sensitive and careful observer. A fuller understanding of these genres may be easier for an insider, but even an outsider who had stayed in northern Japan longer would have been able to see that the farmers were making annual gifts to the local large landowners.

(*b*) Those expressions of everyday life which can be *heard*: regional dialect, figures of speech, occupational terms, village slang, proverbs, lullabies and other songs, tales, jokes, legends, rumors, and gossip. The observer at level (*a*) would be able to see these expressions occurring, but would have almost no idea about meaning unless he or she knew the language—including local usage. The key to level (*b*), then, is language facility; and especially in the case of Japan, this makes (*b*) considerably more complex than (*a*). A non-Japanese with an interpreter could perform on the (*a*) level, but given the cultural aspect of the Japanese language (its vocabulary, grammar, style, and politeness forms are dictated by social position, context, gender, and age), a Japanese researcher would be almost a necessity on level (*b*).

(*c*) Those *beliefs* and nuances of worldview and shared value which are seldom articulated but often couched in taboos or customs or folk ideas (as Alan Dundes has called them). Here the insider has to know the language, but needs as well to appreciate and (as far as Yanagita is concerned) actually share in the phenomenon as it is experienced and believed. The researcher, in other words, must go beyond mere intellectual curiosity and become involved in the localized emotional and cultural milieu in which the belief or custom or story makes sense. Indeed Yanagita insisted that his students submit a subjective description of the traditional event they were documenting—recording their own participation, their thoughts, their reactions, and so on—as substantive proof of their understanding of what had occurred. In modern anthropological terms, the participant-observer, especially if he or she is a member of the culture being studied, must not only acknowledge a close relationship to what is happening, but also consider the internal validity of the event and whether it has been altered by the researcher's presence.

The importance of this apparently introspective aspect of folklore study cannot be understated, for it insists that the researcher recognize his or her involvement in, response to, and use of any folklore. Since all humans employ folklore every day, presumably researchers "have" as much of it as the people they study; so if only the lore of the "informant" is acknowledged, the study becomes lopsided or arrogant. Dimension (*c*) may initially sound "unscientific," for it includes a subjective perspective which science normally pretends to screen out. Indeed many of Yanagita's modern critics fault him for that very reason. But it seems to us that level (*c*) recognizes, along with art and literature and music generally, that a large part of cultural studies actually lies not in the *manifest content* of a story or song or dance or gesture or custom, but in the complex set of shared emotions and values which may be foregrounded and made experiential by skilled expression. To ignore this aspect of communication is surely unscientific, for it is at the core of why people continue to perform traditional genres. Moreover, to overlook, deny, or denigrate this important element of meaning degrades the materials themselves, for a culturally meaningful legend is easily converted into a childish or quaint example of how people expressed themselves "before they became intelligent."

For our own purposes in collaborating on this book, the Yanagita approach has been helpful and illuminating; for while it certainly takes a Japanese person to handle levels (*b*) and (*c*), only an outsider asks the obvious questions which insiders do not need to articulate. In this book, which is addressed to insiders and outsiders alike, we feel that both perspectives (an insider's sense of nuance, an outsider's sensible ignorance) can provide a dialectic interaction resulting in some interesting observations on the materials. If one can approach a Japanese legend with some awareness of the many values out of which it grows and the contexts which give it meaning, one can more fully experience (for Japanese people, reexperience) the elements which constitute the culture.

This phenomenon, as it relates particularly to legends, is extremely important, for it is through the processes of oral tradition that a member of any culture experiences the accumulated past within the present moment. In other words, folk tradition allows us to "take the past along with us," reliving it at every step, rather than leaving it behind like a dead fossil. According to Yanagita, *senzo* (ancestors) are not relatives who have vanished from the scene but personages who continue to exist *because* they are celebrated. Thus our connection to our family and culture is active as well as personal and subjective; probably Yanagita would say that just as we continue to have ancestors as long as we celebrate them, we also have a culture and history as long as we maintain our traditions on all three levels of awareness.

Of course, a number of different genres can be closely analyzed for cultural patterns, but legends are particularly lively because they show no sign of slacking off in oral currency, popularity, or function. While some material crafts become obsolete or rare when they are superseded by new methods, tools, or needs, legends have maintained a striking vitality through the years. In the United States, for example, there seem to be even more legends in circulation now than a hundred years ago (this impression may also be due to increased scholarly interest and publication). In the case of Japan, legends are still popular in both urban and rural contexts, and legends of ghosts being seen, for example, at railroad crossings seem as common nowadays as the older ones where they were spotted near cliffs, rivers, lakes, and mountains. Almost every legend in this book is familiar to a wide range of contemporary Japanese.

We may not be able to account precisely for the undiminished relevance of legends, but certainly their persistence in what we consider to be more sophisticated times indicates that they serve some important function. They seem to dramatize areas of doubt, ambiguity, anxiety, and concern which are not addressed by "scientific" means—matters involving human emotions which are strongly connected to cultural values, but for which there are no clear answers. In any case, as we hope to show, legends are not told simply because we are gullible; this way of viewing them emerges when they are taken out of context and approached only for their entertainment or instructional value. Deprived of cultural context, legends seem superficial or even downright stupid: many schoolchildren unfortunately get their first stereotypes of other peoples by reading or hearing legends which depict American Indians as poor observers of nature ("that's how the bear got a short tail"), rural people as dull ("that's how Levan got its name"), or Japanese people as "superstitious" about ghosts. But, as we noted earlier, legends are not simply *about* something; they are concrete enactments *of* something which otherwise would usually remain an abstraction.

The legend, as a kind of traditional narrative, is an orally performed story which purports to relate something that actually happened, an event which occurred in the same world in which the teller and listener live, but which took place in front of others (often the friend of a friend, in the case of modern "urban" legends, or a deceased relative in the older ones). Unlike the folktale, which is clearly fiction, the legend uses details and a convincing style to create a lifelike account. Even when the teller is not entirely convinced of the "facts," the story will be narrated as if it could be true, as if it were being held up for verification—or at least serious scrutiny.

Unlike a myth, which usually describes the actions of gods, saviors, and other larger-than-life characters, the legend focuses on people like those who are telling and hearing the story; in other words, there is an implied similarity and kinship between the narrators and the characters in their legends, as if the same sort of thing could happen to both of them—and this is how the legend establishes much of its sense of immediacy. Again unlike myth, which usually shows action on a cosmic scale (worlds and universes being created and ordered, nations rising and falling), the legend deals with an occurrence which happened, or could have happened, right in our neighborhood or down the street at a particular well-known location; one result is immediacy and a sense of the possible and plausible.

Yet the action in a legend usually defies or tests everyday logic (though it may illustrate our suspicions or assumptions about what really lies behind the normal course of events). In America, elderly ladies explode their poodles in microwaves, young ladies cook their own innards at tanning salons, children find alligators in the sewers, philandering husbands ask their wives to sell the Porsche and send them the proceeds, teenagers hear the clink of a metal hook on the door handle of their parked car. In Japan, the angry or frustrated ghosts of departed mothers still nurse their coffin-born infants, strange phenomena occur in deserted temples, foxfire is seen in graveyards, small combs fall from the beams of a house where a child was murdered, and so on. These stories are set in the everyday world, but their content is not as cozy and comforting as one expects routine reality to be; and that perhaps is one of their functions, for daily life is seldom what we wish or suppose.

Beyond that, with a bit of literary acumen, we can usually ask the kinds of questions which will lead us closer to the community values that are being dramatized in the narrative of a legend. A fairly well-known legend in Oregon relates how two of the early settlers got into a heated discussion over what to name the newly founded principal town. One, who came from Boston, Massachusetts, wanted to name the town Boston; the other, from Portland, Maine, held out for his hometown. According to the legend, which is known to practically every schoolchild in the state, the two men tossed a coin and let this gamble decide the issue—in this instance on behalf of Portland.

Now it may very well be that the incident (or something like it) actually happened; calling it a legend does not call its factuality into question. But we want to know why *this* occurrence, out of many that must have taken place that day, that week, that month in the exciting and burgeoning Northwest, why this story became the one consistently passed down to account for "how Portland got its name."

Looking at the story as a piece of literature, we notice that the two characters are white, and that it is apparently males who are deciding what to call places in the Northwest. We note that both of them come from New England and both want to name the new town not after the local Indians (as settlers in nearby Washington usually did), but after their own regional origins: for them—as for their descendants— naming the land had to do with establishing something New Englandish in the far Northwest. Moreover, we see that the legend shows the dilemma being solved not by elected officials, democratic vote, referendum, or petition, but by the expedient of the tossed coin—nicely in keeping with the gambler's mood which brought many of the early New England traders and merchants into the Northwest in the first place.

In other words, just reviewing the literary suggestions of the narrative, we find this otherwise simple and mundane anecdote constitutes a veritable tableau scene of the assumed values which did indeed underlie the early settlement of the Pacific Northwest. Next to the nuances of this legend, its factual content recedes into relative unimportance. If the incident did not happen as described, it should have; for the image of speculation, colonialization, and exploitation by white males in the Northwest certainly reflects the feeling by which Oregon established and differentiated itself from nearby states.

Mothers and Children

In "Kasamatsu Pass and Turtle Rock," we have a similar kind of legend, for on the surface it seems only to be a rather fantastic story about how a turtle-shaped rock got its name— not, after all, a very exciting issue (why not simply say that the rock looks like a turtle, and so people named it that?). The legend as narrated uses the rock and the striking events which are said to have occurred there to bring together a cluster of meaningful cultural truths: a mother protects her young with her life, the intensity of her dedication still affects the place and those who come near it, and the stone remains to remind us of the values which animate the story—just as Portland persists to recall the displacement of Indian by white and the replacement of western wilderness with New England cultivation.

KASAMATSU PASS AND TURTLE ROCK

When you pass over the Bōzukorobashi Bridge and then head off in the direction of Tokura village, along the way—on the right, above a low pass—you go by a village called Kurosaki. There's an old pine tree that grows in this village—it looks like an open umbrella—and people call the pass Kasamatsu, "Umbrella Pine."

Near this low pass, in fact right there on the ocean shore, stands a huge stone that people call Kamenoko-Ishi, "Turtle Rock." This stone really looks like a turtle with a shell about as big as a room of ten *tatami*.

A long time ago, a huge turtle came up on this shore to lay her eggs. The beach was steep and hard to climb, and so she really had to work at it. At the last moment, a giant serpent came along and attacked the turtle, but because of her thick armor, he couldn't do anything to her. I guess the turtle was worried about her eggs because she stayed there for months, just sitting tight on the shore, to protect them inside her body, because the serpent watched her constantly and just waited to get at the eggs. Finally—so they say—she turned into a stone. And later the serpent slithered across the water in the direction of the Mito shore not far from Tokura village.

Even today, so the story goes, when the strong winds blow and the sea gets wild, the trail of that giant serpent can be seen stretching across from Kamenoko-Ishi to the Mito shore. The color of the seawater around Turtle Rock changes seven times a day. And on the third and seventh anniversary of this turtle's death, several people were drawn so irresistibly into the ocean there that they drowned. For that reason, the local people fear this place as if it was cursed. Also last summer, I heard that a young woman fell into the water there and drowned.[1]

Many legends end with an apparently factual element which really functions less as explanation than as a reference to a material object or place, the existence of which is a constant reminder (perhaps "proof") of the story and its attendant values. A Native American story that ends, "That's how coyote got yellow eyes," does not really explain why coyotes have yellow eyes, but instead refers to a feature which everyone will see numerous times during a lifetime. Then the sight of the familiar characteristic will recall the situation in the story where selfishness or betrayal or mishandling of his own body accounts for the way the coyote looks today. The values being expressed relate to the dangers of selfishness, betrayal, and misbehavior and not primarily to what a coyote resembles.

Similarly a Japanese legend might end, "That's why there is an Inari shrine on that spot," but the story may only partly explain the establishment of the shrine. Inari is not simply the depiction of a fox, but a reference to a complex of beliefs and religious customs which are brought up and illustrated by the story. Here Turtle Rock is a familiar place, and its presence in the community reminds people constantly of the story. The legend, it seems clear, functions like a cameo of cultural meaning; in it, image, symbol, plot, internal logic, and characterization work as referents to cultural values and abstract ideas which underlie the story.

A WEEPING STONE

Along the path through the mountains near Sayo-no-Nakayama on Honshū, there is a stone that you can hear crying and complaining. A long time ago, people found a pregnant woman traveler dead and robbed on that spot. The murderer was never caught, and so the killing remained unresolved and unatoned for. The unlucky spirit of the dead woman could never find any rest, and finally took refuge in that stone. Every night she weeps because of her grief. You can still hear her crying.[2]

Sayo-no-Nakayama lies in Kakegawa-shi in Shizuoka Prefecture. The motif of a stone or cliff that weeps or talks to passersby, or gives off remarkable and inexplicable noises is found widely in Japan. Since such stones are now usually identified as highway deities (*sae-no-kami*) which protect travelers, the legend may well represent the development of a local inhabiting spirit into a generalized deity. But even more important, this legend is immediately recognizable as a member of the large body of *ubume* stories which dramatize the plight of an undefended pregnant woman. The theme is extremely widespread in Japanese folklore, popular culture, and art and is one of many such clusters of meaning which are richly suggestive.

We are accustomed to this richness on the elite level. For example, we are well acquainted with the fact that a haiku implies more than it says; often a single word in the haiku can suggest time of day or season of the year to the reader who is attuned to the nuances of the form. Similarly, in *ikebana* each element in a flower arrangement has a meaning that goes beyond the appearance of the individual flowers. On the traditional level, it is much the same, although some people may be reluctant to accord to everyday culture the same richness and complexity. In woodblock prints, in customary arts and crafts, in the traditional folding of paper birds, for example, there are meanings which are not overtly articulated and therefore exist not in the items themselves, but in the minds and values of those who use them. A string of paper birds may seem to an outsider a puzzling, but cute, item to hang on the children's memorial at Hiroshima; but to someone who knows the imagery and meaning of *senbazuru* (a thousand cranes, with the cranes representing longevity and the number one thousand indicating intensity and power) and recognizes the exacting labor of folding all those pieces of paper, the offering becomes a moving tribute to children who perished and simultaneously a commitment to continue to celebrate them. Here again, the meaning does not inhere in the string of birds itself, but rather in the shared values of those to whom the offering of a thousand cranes makes cultural sense.

This does not imply, however, that everything in legend makes sense in any simple way. Just as some of the world's best-written literature is powerful because it explores life's ambiguities without settling them, many of the most effective legends do not illustrate a single identifiable point but rather strikingly dramatize several juxtaposed or contrary notions at the same time. The *ubume* (or *kosodate*) motif is composed of some very interesting contrasts. For one, the mother has often died in childbirth, thus suggesting that the surviving child is to some extent guilty of her demise. At the same time, a mother has a solid obligation to defend and nurture her child even in death; thus, not only does the child nurse at the breast, but it receives sweets or rice cakes which the mother's ghost provides at considerable expenditure of energy.

UBUME, OR KOSODATE-YŪREI

Some time ago, the wife of a farmer here in Katsurada died of a sudden illness in her last month of pregnancy. During the night of the forty-ninth day after her death, forty-nine *mochi* were discovered missing—funeral rice cakes that people had left in front of the Buddha in the temple. When the villagers became suspicious and took a look at the grave, they discovered a big hole in the side of the burial mound. Now the relatives of the dead woman thought over the rumors that had been going around the neighborhood, and finally decided to dig up the grave in the presence of a village official.

When they dug her up, they found not only that there wasn't any change in the color of her skin but also saw that she was clutching a little baby dressed in funeral clothes. This baby had a curved back, and had a rice cake in his hand and was licking it. Apparently the baby had been born after the woman's burial and had survived somehow.

Now the people wanted to take the baby away from its mother, but she wouldn't let go of the child. After they thought it over, they called for a woman who was still nursing and had her show the dead woman her breast. She told her, "I'll feed your baby with it; you can give your baby to me safely." After the woman said that, the arms of the corpse loosened, and she let go of the child. So people say.

They also say that the people found the rice cakes that had disappeared earlier from the temple. They were there in the coffin, along with six pieces of the carton in which they had been packed. The label was taken to Tōkō Temple in Katsurada and preserved; during the equinox Buddhist services, this label is brought out, and people pray for the salvation of the souls of the dead.[3]

Even on the surface, there is enough to respond to here: two contrasting, but mutually interactive, modes of obligation and guilt are brought together in the same drama. But the case is even more complex, for as the notes to some of these legends point out, the story line itself may go back to

Ubume, a deceased mother caring for her living infant. Artist: Nankai (other information unknown).

an older (but residually persistent) idea that it is the baby who is the powerful and dangerous entity, not the mother's ghost. The baby, born in the grave and thus unritualized as a newcomer (just as the dead mother is often inadequately ritualized because she has died in a strange town or in the mountains), is a potential danger to any passerby, to society, to the world. It is the job of the living to provide the proper ritualized order in which the dead may rest, the living may prosper, and the community (for the time being) will be safe. Thus the story may not only dramatize the obligatory interactions of mother and child but also of the living and the dead—which are both concerns which engage the Japanese legend audience.

The same theme is encountered in several forms. In the following example, the familiar situation testifies to the unique qualities possessed by a particular legendary monk. If one were to "decode" the story on the most basic level, it seems to dramatize the belief that a properly ritualized person is changed from a potential threat to the society (one who *consumes* the ritual offerings) to one who brings blessings and success. In a way, this story parallels the larger assumptions about the gradual movement of a dead person from dangerous ghost to helpful *kami*.

MOSUKE-INARI

Some time ago, on the last day of the year, a woman traveler was passing the Fukiagedera Temple in the city of Wakayama and fell dead in the street, right there in front of the temple. Even though she was simply dressed, she looked somehow to be from a higher class. And she was in the last month of pregnancy. Out of compassion for this poor dead woman, the priest of the temple chanted a sutra for her and buried her in the Fukiagedera graveyard.

A few days after that, an unknown woman began appearing every night in a nearby confectionery store to buy candies. The woman came to the store exactly at the same time, but always late in the night, just as the owner wanted to go to bed. The shopkeeper eventually began to wonder about it, and watched the woman secretly.

One night the woman arrived, just as she had before. She bought her candy and went happily along her way. The owner stared after her for a while, but when he looked casually into the money box, he didn't see the *mon* coin that the woman had given him—instead all he saw was a leaf from a tangerine tree. So right away he followed after her. But when he got to the wall near the Fukiagedera Temple, she disappeared without a trace.

The shopkeeper was stunned by all this, and went right back home. Next day, he went to the temple and told the priest what he had seen the night before. The priest was also curious about it, and went with the storekeeper to the grave of that woman traveler. The priest had his servant dig up the grave, and as they brought the coffin up, they could hear a baby crying. They took off the coffin lid as fast as they could, and there they found a newborn baby boy who was sucking on a piece of *ame* candy. They were struck by such mother love as that. Even after death, she had been trying to give sweets to her baby.

Later the child was raised by this priest, who named him Mosuke. The people in that area called him "Ghost Mosuke." While he lived, he was a believer in Inari, the rice god. He could run unusually fast, too. When he died, people made a figurine that looked like him, put it in an Inari shrine, and worshipped him there. Sometime after that, they began to call this shrine "Mosuke-Inari." People who had afflictions of the feet or legs, or mothers who lacked enough milk—people like that prayed to this Inari all the time. People believed that he would fulfill their request right away.[4]

Inari is often described as a goddess who rules over the five cereal grains. She is also called Uga-no-mitama and may be the same as the fertility goddess Toyo-uke-hime; as a god of harvest, Inari also appears as male. Inari-Shinkō is the widespread belief system for which the Fushimi Shrine in Kyoto provides the home base. The Inari Festival fits in neatly with the agricultural observances of both spring and fall, suggesting that Inari-Shinkō has developed from a fusion of two sets of beliefs or ritual occasions. One of these is centered on the field deity itself, Ta-no-kami (*ta* is field), which was originally identical to the ancestral deity (*sorei*). Ta-no-kami comes from the mountains in the spring and returns in the fall after the harvest. The other set focuses on the fox as a messenger of Inari. The many Inari temples in Japan are guarded by two stone foxes, and this custom has led many Japanese today to believe that the fox itself is the rice god.

Since the Middle Ages, Inari-Shinkō has become very popular in Japan, and the agrarian power of Inari is still very much accepted; in addition, the concept has been adopted and adapted in a number of situations where "fertility" is important but unpredictable, for example, in fishing villages and among business people. Many Japanese who report no active religious affiliation note that those in the family who are in business visit the Inari shrines regularly to pray for success in their undertakings.

On the narrative level, this legend illustrates the ideal that a mother's obligation to nurture and protect her child is not dissolved by death (in a similar vein, in "The Ghost of the Tofu Seller's First Wife," the *yūrei* of the first wife returns to kill the second wife, who has been mistreating her orphaned child). There is also the older belief, suggested in the preceding *ubume* legend, that the unborn fetus or the unritualized baby of a dead mother is dangerous and thus must be dealt with. Properly ritualized or mollified, the child may grow up with remarkable speed and possessed of unique powers which testify to his strange origins.

Thus, in traditional Japan, when a person was especially gifted (in this case with great vigor and running ability), or was born with an exceptional mark like white hair, a rumor might circulate that he had been "born in the grave of his mother." The particular abilities would become, as in this case, an iconic way of recalling the person and referring to a quality which visitors to a shrine might want to obtain for themselves. Here a votive figure of Mosuke-Inari not only serves as a visual reminder of the story (and thus its moral import) but becomes a religious focal point for those who have sickness of the legs and feet or mothers who lack sufficient breast milk. Art as a visual reminder or token of the story's meaning is found in several other legends in this collection and is a common motif.

The theme is so well known that it can also be used to "explain" the existence of a painting or print or Kabuki play motif. The following version concentrates not so much on the fate of the child and its mother, but on the task of "getting a picture" of the apparition—clearly a far more complicated matter in the days before the camera.

OBLIGATIONS OF A DEAD MOTHER

Once someone knocked on the front door of a confectioner's shop in the Yasuhara area of the Date district between 3:00 and 3:30 in the morning. The shopkeeper got up, and when he opened the door, a woman came in and stood on the earthen floor of the entryway. She looked still young, but her hair hung down straight over her shoulders. She wore a white kimono and carried an apparently newborn baby in her arms. She kept pushing the hair out of her eyes with an angry look, and said that she would like very much to have some sweet *ame* [rice candy], and then paid for it with a *mon* coin [the smallest monetary unit in old Japan]. The shopkeeper sold her the *ame*; she took it, thanked him, and went away.

Again the next night, about the same time and in the same condition, she bought *ame* and went away. The shopkeeper started wondering about it, so one day he talked to an artist who was a good friend of his. The artist was just as puzzled as the shopkeeper and said he would come by that evening so he could see for himself.

So that evening the artist got his brush, some paper, some rice wine and snacks, and visited the confectioner. They drank and talked until late into the night. Then they heard someone knocking on the door. The shopkeeper motioned to the artist to get out of sight, stood up, and went to the door. As he opened it, in came this mysterious woman who wanted *ame* for a *mon*. The shopkeeper intentionally took a long time stirring the *ame* around in the barrel, and the artist hid behind something. From there he was able to draw a picture of the woman.[5]

As in the story of Mosuke, the dead mother tries not only to nourish her surviving baby but to treat him to *ame*, the rice candy so ubiquitous in Japanese children's experience. In earlier times, *ame* was kept in barrels or casks, where the pieces of candy floated in water. This gives the shopkeeper the opportunity to take his time stirring around in the cask while his artist friend creates a picture which stands as a visual confirmation of the experience. Such famous prints as Toyokuni's depiction of the actor Onoe Matsusuke in the role of the murdered woman Iohata trigger responses of recognition among those Japanese who know this story or motif. Many of the ghost paintings owned by the Zenshōan Temple in Tokyo are presented as pictorial records by artists who witnessed the appearance of particular ghosts; the unmistakable visual codes—long (often disheveled) hair, white kimono, lack of feet, a pained or angry expression, tongues of fire nearby—make clear to the viewer that the ghost is culturally authentic, and hence believable (see Ubume picture, p. 65).

Of course, the audience of the legend would know, although the shopkeeper seems not to, that the unbound hair and white dress of the woman identify her as a person who has had a funeral. The woman's consternation is our clue to the deeper meaning in the story: she is troubled because of the unritualized child, and her appearance is meant to call others' attention to the problem. In some other versions of the *ubume* legend, like the following ("A Nighttime Encounter"), the dead mother walks the streets at night, shocking any observer into obtaining the services of a priest (which is exactly what the child needs).

On the surface, such legends illustrate tenderness, love, and motherly responsibility for a child's welfare even after death. On a deeper level, as noted earlier, something far more complex is at work: in older Japanese belief, a fetus (as well as any child less than seven) is very powerful, unpredictable, and potentially dangerous. In Aomori Prefecture in northern Japan, one hears the phrase, *nanasai made wa kami no uchi* (until seven years old, a child belongs to the *kami*), and the spirits of young children are often described as *wakaba no mitama* or *wakaba no rei* (fresh-young-leaves' spirits), testifying to their extra natural vitality. Originally the idea seems to have been that a fetus (dead or alive) retains its primordial vitality; since it is not yet under the control of societal norms, it can constitute a threat to living people. There is a possibility that the connection with blood (during birth) might have suggested ritual uncleanness as well. In northern Japan, there was the custom of separating a dead fetus from a woman who had died pregnant and burying it either folded in her arms or at her back. Either a funeral for a dead fetus, or some adoption process for a live one, has the capacity to bring the child (or its spirit) into the ritual life of the community.

In later times, this fear of the fetus remains in the contemporary funeral rituals for aborted fetuses (*mizuko*, literally "water babies"). Fear or guilt in the story may be dramatized by the mother's attempts to feed the child (much exploited for its sentimental effect in later Kabuki usage), or her unwillingness to loosen her hold until a substitute source of nurturance is assured. The survival of the child on rice cakes from the funeral altar in the earlier story not only calls attention to the dead mother's dilemma but also emphasizes the liminal situation of the child, for normally a living person would not partake of funeral offerings. As noted in Part II, the number forty-nine signifies the number of days involved in the basic funeral observance. As in many other legends, the story and its values can be brought vividly to mind through the iconic reference to a picture or item displayed in a temple or shrine.

As suggested by these examples, there are three rather large categories of legends associated with this theme of the liminal fetus:

(*a*) One type focuses on the child entirely, usually detailing the erection of memorial stones for children who were drowned, murdered, or aborted. The stone weeps until people hold proper ceremonies with sufficient reading of sutras. Usually the area around such stones is considered very dangerous.

(*b*) Another category is characterized by a fixed sequence of motifs which include the sudden death and burial of a pregnant woman, her appearance at a confectionery shop at the same time every night to buy candy (or her repeated appearance in someone's dream to announce that a child has been born in a nearby grave), the pursuit of the woman by a suspicious observer and her subsequent disappearance into a cemetery, the excavation of her grave and discovery of the dead woman with a male child in her arms, and the adoption and raising of the child, who becomes a famous Buddhist monk.

(*c*) In another type, a woman carries a newborn baby whom she tries to hand to passersby as a kind of test. If the baby is accepted, it immediately becomes heavier and heavier until the person can hardly hold it. If the person nonetheless succeeds, he (less often, she) is asked to state a wish and is usually rewarded with some supernormal power. But the recipient must remember to hold the child facing its mother; otherwise the baby will lean forward and bite through the person's throat, killing him or her. The following is a related example:

A NIGHTTIME ENCOUNTER

One rainy night about midnight, a young man from Hashirada village was on his way home through the lonely streets. He had been drinking sake in a tavern on the edge of town. His head started to clear as he walked through the light rain, and as he went along, he sang a little song. Suddenly, behind him, he thought he heard a small child crying. He stopped and listened. "Who's coming along here at this time of night letting a child cry?" he wondered, and decided to wait for the people and walk along with them.

So he stood there, waiting. As the crying came closer, he looked around and saw a strange-looking woman with unkempt hair and white clothing walking toward him. She was carrying a child in her arms. He stood and stared at her as if he was rooted to the spot, and the strange woman walked quickly by.

As soon as he saw that she was headed in the direction of Hashirada village, though, he came to his senses and followed her. Besides, this forbidden fruit really attracted him; or maybe he was enchanted by her. He caught up to her just as she reached the cemetery by Tōkōji Temple in Hashirada. Just then she turned around and smiled at him, and thousands of bright sparks flamed up all around her. She disappeared into the smoke, and the young man fell unconscious on the ground. The priest of this temple found him there the next morning, and was able to bring him back to consciousness and take him home.[6]

It is possible that the young man falls unconscious from fright, but the fact that he is earlier struck motionless, then—in spite of the woman's obvious *yūrei* looks (flowing hair and white kimono)—is drawn to follow her, indicates that his condition results from her powerful spirit attraction, which acts upon him like a psychological attack. So traumatic is the encounter that the young man must be rescued later by a priest. It is so unlikely, according to Japanese custom, that anyone would be wandering through the streets at night with a crying baby that the young man probably ought to have taken a hint and averted his eyes (in which case, of course, there would have been no story to pass on to us).

Most of these *ubume* stories share with the *zashiki-warashi* legends (discussed later in this chapter) a concentration on the child, not the mother, as the central figure, indicating the danger and worry posed by a young child thought to possess exceeding amounts of unchanneled energy. In the following legend, the major concern of the deceased mother is comforting her baby rather than ritual matters, but the same intense solicitude for the child, coupled with an appeal to the living for help, dramatizes the interactive responsibilities understood to exist between the realms of the living and the dead.

THE GHOST OF THE TOFU SELLER'S FIRST WIFE

Once there was a temple called Shōmeiji, which stood behind the Tenmangū Shrine at Ushioe (it's become the Hōtoku School since then). There were a lot of cemeteries in that area, and only a few people lived nearby, so naturally it was very lonely there, both day and night. The people used to say that a ghost would appear in front of this temple night after night, and a brave man named Yamada wanted to go and check this out with two of his friends. So he went over there.

In the evening, they came to the temple. They sat on a bridge over a brook to while away the time. About midnight, they saw something strange coming closer in the darkness under the bridge. Yamada's two friends were so scared that they said they felt like their souls had jumped out of their bodies. Then Yamada told them that for the past few minutes, someone under the bridge had been holding tightly to his legs with cold hands. The other two were terrified, and got out of there without saying any more.

Now only Yamada remained. As he pulled up each hand that held his legs, he could make out the figure of a grieving woman dressed in white clothing. She had wild, flowing hair. He asked her who she was, why she had come there, and why she was hanging onto his ankles. The strange woman answered that she had been the wife of a tofu seller who lived in the neighborhood. She had died before her husband, and he had married again. But that second wife had a bad temper, and she was tormenting the first one's child.

So the first wife had gone back home to do something about it. But she couldn't get into the house because an *ofuda* [a small folded paper talisman] was fastened to the doorway. She wanted to ask a passerby to get rid of the *ofuda* for her, but everyone who saw her got scared and left right away, so now she didn't know what to do. So she asked Yamada to have pity on her, and to do her a favor and remove that paper amulet.

Yamada agreed to help out and went along with her. As soon as he took the *ofuda* from the door of the tofu seller's house, the woman smiled happily and slipped through the doorway. She had hardly gone in when Yamada heard a woman scream. Yamada said later that this second wife was bewitched by the ghost of the first wife, and was frightened to death.[7]

While revenge is certainly the central focus, this legend also dramatizes the function of the *ofuda*, or protective paper amulet which is fastened to the house doorway to keep out the spirits of the dead. In this story, the removal of an *ofuda* by a living person allows the ghost to enter the house and complete its revenge (which, though out of sight, appears to be effective). Boundaries or thresholds of one sort or another (crossroads, bridges, doorways, riverbanks) are typical of the critical intersections where ghosts may be encountered and repelled; thus many ghost legends are set in these meeting places to heighten dramatic action and create "pregnant" situations where the living are most likely to connect with the dead.

Like the fetus, the spirit of a child who has died may also be dangerous, or at least more powerful than anything local people can handle without ritual. Like the European kobold, the *yūrei* of a child can positively influence a household if it has been properly dealt with; otherwise its effects can be catastrophic, capricious, scary. The *zashiki-warashi* (*zashiki* means room, and *warashi* is a small child) stories are found mostly in northern Japan, where in earlier times, it was apparently the custom to dispose of aborted fetuses or children killed shortly after birth under the earthen floor of the kitchen. The *yūrei* appears as a child about three to ten years old with a distinctive haircut. It manifests itself by making a noise, or dropping a common object where it can be seen by others. Usually this ghost is visible only to children. Sometimes the *zashiki-warashi* steals someone's pillow, and sometimes it climbs on a sleeping person and presses the chest (which indicates that the universal "Hag" dream discussed by David Hufford in *The Terror That Comes in the Night* is interpreted in Japan according to culturally shared values, as we would expect). Otherwise the *zashiki-warashi* is not necessarily dangerous, as long as it is properly ritualized and mollified.

A LITTLE GIRL'S HOUSE GHOST

About twenty members of a clan once gathered at the house of Lord Shōnosuke of Hiishi in the village of Tsuchibuchi. It was on the evening of the twenty-ninth day of the ninth month. As they ate *mochi* together to celebrate the harvest festival, a tiny woman's comb fell suddenly from the open beam above them. Everybody was amazed, and wondered what it could be. They looked up, but they couldn't see anything. A few of them thought they saw the face of a girl with loose flowing hair who was holding onto the beam and staring down at them.

I heard this right from an old man who was there at that time and saw it himself. People said it was the ghost of a little girl who had died of hunger during a famine year. Her ghost still lives up in the beams of that house.[8]

TWO CHILD HOUSE GHOSTS

A similar child's ghost lived on the beams of a house with the Yamashita family of Kyude in Aza-Tochinai in that same village. Once the villagers had come together in this house for Nenbutsukō. As they began to chant the Nenbutsu prayer, "Gaki no Nenbutsu nam'maida," a child's voice also spoke, "Gaki no Nenbutsu nam'maida." When the people down below said, "Namu Amidabutsu," the child up above on the beam also said, "Namu Amidabutsu."

The people were frightened about it, they say. This child was killed during the Temmei era because of his thievish tendencies—or something like that—by being locked in a room and suffocated with steam. The soul of this child behaved just like a house ghost, and often scared visitors. So they say.

During the famine time in the Ten'mei Period [1781–88] in Yamaguchi, in that same village of Tsuchibuchi, there was a thieving child in the Yakushidō family. Because the people of the village often complained about this child, his family and relatives finally got together and tried to figure out what to do. They decided that the father should take the child into the mountains and kill him with an ax after he had fallen asleep from exhaustion up on the cliffs.

So the father took this child along with him into the mountains, telling him they were going to cut wood. They climbed far up into the cliffs, and after a while the young boy begged to sit down and rest. Soon he was asleep, and his father tried to figure out the quickest way to kill him. As he raised his ax to strike his child in the head, though, the boy awoke, jumped up, and said, "Father, what are you trying to do?" His father answered him, "You'll find that out in the other world!" lifted his ax again, and drove it into the boy's head.

They say that the boy's soul returned to his home, has stayed there ever since up in the beams of the house, and keeps repeating sadly that last question: "Father, what are you trying to do?" So they say.[9]

There is good evidence that infanticide was practiced in Japan in response to famines (either on practical grounds of reducing the number of mouths to feed, or on the psychological bases which have surfaced in times of great cultural stress). Stealing of food was no doubt common during famines, but at the same time, it was considered morally wrong; children were killed, but at the same time, they were supposed to be protected and nurtured. Thus infanticide, even when motivated by economic factors, must have produced anxiety, guilt, and fear.

This legend thus juxtaposes cultural values of two potentially conflicting sorts: family stability, in which children are central, and community stability, in which individuals and families are subordinated to the collective well-being. The Japanese proverb, "The nail that sticks up will get hammered down," has its price: the resultant guilt among those who have sacrificed their children's naïveté to the demands of community harmony is appropriately articulated by the boy's poignant, "Father, what are you trying to do?" "Gaki no Nenbutsu nam'maida" is a prayer associated with the spirit of hunger, and *Namu Amidabutsu* is an incantation to summon Amida Buddha. The *Nenbutsukō* is a group which meets to recite Buddha's name.

A legend like this thus dramatizes the juxtaposition of deep cultural values with an immediate emergency and

The ghost of a prostitute named Hototogisu (Cuckoo), in the Kabuki play Keisei Asamagadake. *Artist: Matsumoto Fūkō (1839–1923).*

The ghost
of Utagawa
Shigesumi, who
saved his infant
son from the Ōtaki
waterfall at Jūnisō
(a neighborhood
in the Shinjuku
section of Tokyo).
The theme is taken
from a story,
"Kaidan Chibusa-
enoki," written
and performed by
Encho himself.
Artist: Itō Seiu
(other information
unknown).

Kohada Koheiji, the murdered husband in a famous Kabuki play. Artist: Ichiunsai Kunitoshi (other information unknown).

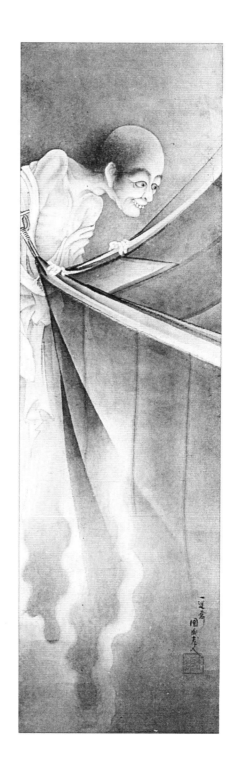

A woman's ghost holding the severed head of a man in her arms. Artist: Kawakami Tōgai (1827–1881), a painter who used the European style at the end of the Edo period and beginning of the Meiji.

A half-kneeling ghost leans against a decorative column; this ghost has feet. Artist: Iijima Kōga (other information unknown).

moral, as well as physical, stress. The inherited sense of guilt from the earlier situation is made continually experiential through the repeated question of the child built into the legend's narration. Gaki, the name of the hunger spirit, is also used in the vernacular to refer to children (who are always hungry). The comb (*kushi*) often appears in connection with ghosts, for its constituent syllables are powerful puns: *ku* (suffering) and *shi* (death).

In a culture in which children are highly prized but infanticide has been prominent; in which people on all levels of life practice interactive relationships which involve deep obligations; in which parental and filial duties are not limited to "this world"; in which rituals are viewed as more efficacious than personal effort or individual opinion, legends such as the ones in this small collection dramatize a stunning array of problems, frustrations, ambiguities, and ironic contrasts. That these ambiguities remain far from resolved in today's world is amply illustrated by contemporary custom and tradition in Japan, as shown in Part II. The questions and anxieties faced by pregnant women in contemporary Japan are perhaps more "modern," but no less burdensome: abortion being legal, but contraceptive pills illegal, Japanese women and their families continue to cope with culturally familiar moral and psychological conflicts, as verified by the growing celebration of the *mizuko kuyō* (a memorial service for the aborted fetus)—one of the most expensive of ceremonies—to atone for the deaths of children and potential children. Since the spirit of any relative may become an ancestor after death, these rituals not only memorialize the deaths of fetuses and infants, but also attempt to ensure the longevity, stability, and success of the family line.

The familiar motif of a mother caring for her child appears in the next legend as a situation which can be remedied only by the reading of sutras in a Buddhist ceremony. The restless soul (here restless because of her concern for her child) is pacified by the sutras, an illustration of the efficacy of normal funeral observances. As a soul makes its way to *anoyo*, the "other side," it remains in the vicinity for a time, and the reading of sutras is thought to ease its passage and help it reach Buddhahood.

THE FIDELITY OF A MOTHER'S SPIRIT

Once there was a man named Heisuke in Nishimachi [the west side] in the village of Yamada in the Kami district. Seven months after his wife had borne him a daughter, she died of an unknown illness. Heisuke was very poor, and had no money to hire a wet nurse. So he carried his child at his own breast, received milk from another mother who gave it to him, and managed to get through each day. But every night about 2:00 A.M., the child began to cry uncontrollably, and Heisuke finally didn't know what to do.

At the same time, there lived a man named Shirobei in Higashimachi [the east side] in the same village. He was a very good person, and when he heard about Heisuke's troubled situation, he felt sympathetic. At that time, he heard someone mention that a flame had been seen coming out of Heisuke's wife's grave. Shirobei went secretly up the burial hill one night and watched, and about 2:00 A.M., a lot of phosphorescent lights flamed up on the grave, and soon there appeared a female ghost in white clothing, and the shining lights became dimmer. He followed this ghost into Yamada village, and as she got to Heisuke's house, Shirobei suddenly heard the baby cry. He felt the dead woman must still feel love for her child.

When he told Heisuke about it the next day, he was very happy, and asked a priest of the temple to perform a funeral service for his dead wife. The priest read sutras and informed her that she didn't need to worry about her child. After that, the baby stopped crying in the night. That's what they say.[10]

Although the reading of sutras is a common ingredient of Japanese Buddhist funeral ceremonies, Buddhism was not originally concerned with the dead; as it moved into Japan, however, its rituals began to incorporate the local obligations performed by the living for the dead. The Buddhist sutras, for example, are said to soothe the anxious *yūrei* which, according to earlier Japanese belief, is thought to remain near the place of its death for a number of days—even years, and may aspire either to Buddhahood or to becoming a local *kami*.

Revenge and Anger

THE GHOST OF A YOUNG GIRL

The daughter of a tofu seller once lived in Nishimachi in Kōrimachi, in the Date district. At the beginning of the year when she became seventeen, she went to a girlfriend's house to visit and was entertained with rice wine. She came back home a little drunk. Because it was chilly, she warmed herself by the sunken fireplace in the center of the room and immediately fell asleep. She was too drunk to notice that the hem of her dress caught on fire while she slept. When she finally woke up and jumped in terror out of the fireplace area, half of her body was already in flames. The crazed girl jumped into the garden pond. After that, pained by water and fire, she lay in her bed seriously ill.

Her girlfriend heard about it and visited her, and spoke to her as consolingly as she could. But the girl in bed only looked at the nicely done hair of her girlfriend. Although her friend spoke with all the possible words of consolation, it finally got to be too much for the sick girl who only stared at her friend's hair and said, "Oh, I envy you that you can have your hair done so beautifully! But I'll soon die!" So the friend departed quickly and went back home.

Two or three days later, the wife of a priest at the Kōri Temple was working alone in her kitchen, and during the absence of the priest, she got thinking about the girl, since a woman in the city had told her, "I hear the tofu seller's daughter will die soon." At this moment, she thought she heard light footsteps, as if someone had come through the temple gate. Then it seemed to her that she heard someone go further into the main hall of the temple and pray. After a while, the person came to the living room of the priest, opened the door, and came in. The woman found the tofu seller's daughter there. She wore a nice new kimono and had her hair carefully done up. She came up to the priest's wife and greeted her politely. The girl's face and voice were hardly those of a sick person.

The woman had her doubts about it, but wanted anyway to invite the girl to tea. When she went into the kitchen to get the dishes and came back, the girl who had been there just a moment before had disappeared and wasn't to be found anywhere. The woman was amazed, and shook as if cold water had been poured down her back. At this moment, a man came from the city and brought the news that the tofu seller's daughter had just died.

On the next day, the body of the girl was buried in the graveyard behind the temple. Early the same evening, as her girlfriend talked to her family about the unlucky fate of the dead girl, the paper hairband that she had just used to do up her hair fell apart.

Later that same night, people heard the scream of a woman in the main hall of Kōri Temple, and wild footsteps, as if someone were running back and forth. When the priest woke his assistant and they went into the hall together, they found the girl who had been buried behind the temple the day before running up and down. The priest and his assistant began to read a sutra together, and after a while the ghost of the girl got tired and disappeared.

On the next night, and the next, the same ghost tore apart the paper hairband in the girlfriend's hair, and came back to the main hall of the temple and ran around everywhere. The priest and his assistant continued to read sutras every night, but it was seven nights before the ghost finally disappeared. That's what they say.

To this day, there's still a piece broken out of the altar railing of the Kōri Temple where the girl's ghost ran through it. That's what people say.[11]

CHŪTA'S GHOST

A farmer named Chūta once lived in Shimogōri in Datezaki village in the Date district. When he died and the people arranged the funeral ceremonies, his corpse became a ghost and flew away over the casket.

One evening in late autumn, when it gets dark quickly outside, seven or eight children were practicing their writing in a corner of the main hall of the temple. Suddenly a shudder went through the room. At the same moment, a bright light flamed up right near the corner where the children were, and the figure of a person appeared hazily in the smoke. The children felt more dead than alive, and put their heads down on the table in fear. A young man among them named Yohei laid his brush down, climbed over the writing table, and ran into the priest's living quarters to tell him what had happened.

The priest stood up and grumbled to himself, "Has Chūta shown up again? The rain must have been annoying him." He opened his umbrella, went back into the main hall of the temple with the boy, and read sutras. After a while, when he put the umbrella down, it flew back and forth and everywhere in the hall. And finally the umbrella landed on the *tatami* floor as if someone had thrown it there. But after that, such an incident never happened again, so they say.[12]

One of the characteristics of Japanese gods is that they help and protect people (mainly the people of their own family and locale) as long as they are properly honored and consistently celebrated with fitting rituals. Yanagita calls these gods *matsurareru kami*, "gods who are celebrated." When the proper honors and rituals are not forthcoming, the gods can quickly change to angry, dangerous, and vengeful; the same emotions are expressed by the spirit of anyone who is unjustly killed.

In many stories, insects appear as a dramatic accompaniment to the *goryō*, the deified vengeful spirit of a martyred person. The intensity and thoroughness with which the insects devour everything, or destroy a local staple crop, are physical signs of the all-consuming nature of the angry *shiryō* (soul). Arising strongly in the Heian Period (794-1185 A.D.), the belief in *goryō* reflected the idea that the spirits of powerful and noble people who had died as victims or martyrs could wreak lifetime revenge upon their antagonists. Since this retaliation could affect others in the vicinity, the custom arose of retaining mountain priests or shamanesses to exorcise the angry spirits and protect the living from the dead. In time, this interaction between local people and shamans seems to have broadened the phenomenon, until common people also could become *goryō* if their deaths were caused by betrayal, torture, or breach of social codes. Anyone who dies under great emotional stress creates an energy which is not easily dissipated; these *yūrei*, thus, have an impact on the local environment and are vivid proof of the seriousness of breaking codes.

ZENTOKU BUGS

There was once a wandering monk named Zentoku. On his travels, he was attacked and killed in the village of Kokufu, in Fukui Prefecture near Kyoto.

In that year, the fields in the vicinity of this valley were attacked by a number of plagues, and the people suffered great losses in the harvest. The farmers believed that these infestations were caused by the murdered monk's revenge, and so they called the vermin "Zentoku bugs."

All the valley dwellers got together on account of this plague and discussed what they could do. Finally, they decided to erect a memorial stone for the monk and hold a funeral service in his memory. This took place in the year 1820. From that time to the present, whenever the insects come out, the people have the Nichiren priests of the Chōgenji Temple in Obama hold a funeral service.[13]

It is worth noting that in one of the many versions of the Okiku or Kiku story, the young, pretty housemaid incurs the jealousy of her mistress, who breaks one of the dishes for which Kiku is responsible. Kiku, taking the blame, commits suicide, and her ghost can be heard counting and recounting the dishes; the wife dies insane; insects eat the local plants and are henceforth known as *Okiku-mushi*, "Okiku bugs."

The wandering mountain ascetic, or *yamabushi*, originally specialized in divining and exorcism, and often supported himself by distributing *ofuda*, those paper or wooden amulets used to ward off evil, bad luck, and ghosts. Naturally such a person was thought to possess considerable and perhaps unpredictable powers, and thus the *yamabushi* were as readily feared as respected. In the following legend, the village is in a moral quandary typical of many of the stories in this collection: on the one hand, the villagers ought to give hospitality and support to the wandering monk because he and his powers could help their interests; on the other hand, he practices his powers in such a frightening way that he threatens the local sense of stability and decorum. In parallel fashion, the potatoes which represent one of the most basic sustaining foods in Japan, are blighted. There is another built-in irony: the local village creates a *goryō* by killing off the very shaman who would normally have been hired to protect them from *goryō*.

NANGAKUBŌ, THE MOUNTAIN HERMIT

This happened in Koyama, a poor village in Shigaraki-gō in the Koga district of Ōmi Province, a place surrounded by mountains where people make a living by raising tea and making ceramics. In olden times, a wandering hermit priest named Nangakubō came into this village. He practiced strange and wonderful magical arts supposedly, but did so in the fashion of someone from the Shingon sect. His doings were too strange for the governor of the village, who began to feel some anxiety about it. He thought it might be dangerous to let such a person run around free, so he arrested the hermit and threw him in prison.

But the governor's fear didn't disappear, so he finally decided to kill the priest. When one of the lower officials learned that he was expected to behead the hermit, he was exasperated, but he had to carry out his boss's orders. So he brought Nangakubō to the execution place, which was high up in the mountains in a thick forest, where even in the daytime it was very dark and sinister.

The officer took his sword in his hand and yelled out purposely loud: "You! Nangakubō! You are a terrible hermit! Because you have been confusing the people's minds, we have to kill you! But this is the order from the governor. If you want to have revenge on anybody, it should be directed at the governor. We lower officials have nothing to do with it!"

Then Nangakubō the hermit raised his head, looked at the official, and said, "Do you not know: when a servant goes out to cut bamboo in the early morning on orders from his master, whose feet will get wet with the dew?" The official turned his face away. Nangakubō spoke again: "When your families plant sweet potatoes, from generation to generation the flowers will bloom on the vines, but no potatoes will grow. Your families will never prosper!" After that he spoke some sort of magical words, prepared himself, and took the posture in which he awaited his death. The official was even more afraid of him now, and beheaded him quickly and resolutely with one stroke.

Later that year, the villagers were plagued by famine and severe sickness, and people spoke about the curse of Nangakubō. They held funeral services for him by the Hōzōji Temple, and built a pagoda next to his grave. They even set up a memorial stone by the road and had "Namu Amidabutsu" engraved on it.

Even so, from the next year on, in the gardens of the lower officials, there grew only sweet potato plants which bore blossoms like those that bloom in the morning breeze, but produced no potatoes on the roots. Even today, sweet potatoes planted by the descendants are unfruitful and bear only blossoms, and strangely, these families have never come to prosperity. The people of this village call the blossoms "Nangaku-bana," and think that they bring bad luck.[14]

People often seek an explanation for extraordinary exceptions to the norm. In the next legend, bamboo, known for its ability to grow tall and straight, grows upside down due to the *goryō* of the murdered monk (when someone murders a monk, norms are reversed and dishonored). The people who live nearby, to pacify the soul of the monk and reduce the effect of his *goryō*—even though they were not involved in his death—name a bridge after him, which still can be seen. The legend thus includes that familiar reference point in the daily lives of the tradition bearers which acts as a physical reminder of the incident, and an explanation of an apparent oddity. The name of the bridge combines -*bashi* / -*hashi* (bridge) and *bōzu* (monk) with *korobashi* (to let someone fall) a nice wordplay.

THE BLIND MONK WITH THE BAMBOO STAFF

The following event took place on an old road that was once called Rikuzen-Tōhamakaidō before the present-day prefectural road was built. In this area, there's a place called Hayashiku that lies only a short distance from the city. In the olden days, a rich, blind monk was making his way along this road and came to this village. A robber with evil on his mind was following him secretly, and as the monk traveled along a lonesome part of the road, the bad man jumped him suddenly to rob him of his money.

The monk protected himself against the robber with a stick made of fresh bamboo. Finally, they fought at close quarters, and the monk drove his stick into a hill nearby and wrestled with the scoundrel. But the blind man could not fight for long. His money was taken away, and he himself was thrown off the cliff. The monk was dead.

But his anger wanted to remain alive in his bamboo stick. So afterward a bamboo thicket grew on that place where the monk had stuck his staff into the ground. All the branches of this tree grew strangely toward the ground, not toward heaven. Because of that, the people called it *sakasadake*—"bamboo that grows upside down."

As a memorial to this monk and to pacify him, the people built a small shrine in the bamboo thicket and dedicated it also to the god who protects against inner-ear infections. Even today there are believers who climb up to this little shrine with thick bamboo cups full of spring water and offer the fresh water to the protective deity.

A short distance from this thicket, there remains the place where the blind monk was thrown off the cliffs. Because a bridge, part of the newer prefectural highway, crosses the canyon there, it's called Bōzukorobashi—and people have carved the words into its parapets.[15]

The following legend overturns two equally important ideal assumptions: first, monks do not drink to excess (partly because, as illustrated in the narrative, it interferes with their vocation); and monks do not kill (even when doing so would rid them of an "improper" influence). Here the monks' frustration has a similar outcome to the killing of a child during a famine year; the story creates a dramatic field of tension, an impossible moral dialectic, between juxtaposed cultural values. The result is a remarkable or unusual occurrence, a favorite situation for the appearance of an angry *yūrei* or for *goryō*, for no matter how or why a person is killed, if he dies angry, his *yūrei* has the power to seek revenge on anything and anyone in the vicinity, for as long as seven generations. The story is a dramatization of values, not a warning about what happens if monks drink.

THE ALCOHOLIC MONK

In northern Japan, they tell of a powerful monk who was an alcoholic. This monk was a great friend of sake. He was often drunk, and when he was drinking, he was not only strong, but got violent and angry with everybody, especially two of his fellow monks.

Finally, they wouldn't take it anymore, so they decided to kill him. They got him totally drunk on rice wine and then dragged him to the edge of a steep cliff at the nearby seacoast. There they threw him over. But when he fell, he grabbed them both and took them with him over the side, and all three smashed into the surf below.

Just then a terrible storm came up, and all the monks of the monastery who had come to the cliffs with the three were badly injured or killed. Every year, on the anniversary of this unlucky event, the same kind of terrible storm comes up. The women of this area, who dive for mussels, believe today that the ghost of that monk resides there at the place where he died, where the water is especially deep, and that he continues to carry out his mischief.[16]

As in the *ubume* legends where a dead mother brings forth a live child, the following narrative presents a striking tableau of life and death: a pregnant woman gives birth and is immediately killed and eaten by wolves. The valorous, but futile, efforts of the priest to avenge the deaths of his wife and child are translated into real phenomena which people in that area still experience: noise in the mountains, local place-names, remarkable (and presumably frightening) occurrences. And, as in the legends where a picture or votive tablet testifies to the occurrence and its importance, the sword may still be seen in a nearby temple. Thus the story acts as not only a dramatization of cultural values and an account which clarifies encounters with the "other world" but also a link with the everyday world in which the listeners and narrators actually live. One could hardly visit Juzu (rosary) or Kesa (surplice) valleys without being reminded of the legend and the deep family emotion it evokes.

On a deeper level, in many rural parts of Japan, there are mixed feelings about the solitude of the mountains: on the one hand, isolation and distance from society foster the spiritual influences sought by the ascetic monk; on the other hand, distance from society also allows for accidents and erosion of those social obligations which characterize the group-centered Japanese way of life. Bodies of murdered persons (and especially those of stillborn, aborted, or murdered children) were disposed of in the mountains; shamed unwed mothers wandered there, as did bandits and banished people (*eta*). Their descendants, called *burakumin*, were excluded from "normal" Japanese society and were often reduced to taking the dishonorable jobs avoided by others—notably disposal and burning of the dead. Thus a legend like this one taps into a great range of assumptions, beliefs, customs, and "culturally loaded" emotions.

In addition, Hori notes that mountains have played a major role in folk religion in Japan, perhaps because some of the influences were brought in from China. Because souls are thought to reside there, the Obon rituals invite the spirits of ancestors from the mountains into the towns and homes and then send them back at the conclusion of the ceremonies. And because this is the abode of souls, many priests wander there; of these, many become shamans (both male and female) whose job it is to protect the living from the angry souls of the dead. Many also develop certain kinds of magic.

The mountains are thus an environment where the living may come into contact with the spirits of the dead, where humans may encounter animals, where wandering priests (*yamabushi*) may intercede between worlds: in short, mountains represent a liminal area where almost anyone is likely to intersect with other dimensions. The following legend thus brings together in one dramatic cluster a number of deeply important images which reflect symbolically on each other.

A MOUNTAIN PRIEST'S FAMILY KILLED BY WOLVES

There is a high mountain called Kumagase-no-mori, broader than one *ri*, near the village of Shatamiai in Makinoyama-gō, in the Kami district. A married couple, both of them wandering priests, were climbing over this mountain years ago. Where they had come from nobody knows, but the wife was in her last month of pregnancy. While they were up on the mountain, she went into labor and had a child. Her husband went back down into the valley to get her some water in his *hora*, a large shell like a snail shell that mountain priests carry.

When he came back, he found that the wolves had eaten his wife and newborn baby. Only their skeletons remained. He began to rave with anger and despair, and drew his sword, and jumped into the midst of the wolf pack. He killed a few of them, but they were too much for one man fighting alone, and finally they ate him, too.

A villager found the sword down in the valley, took it home, and made it his own, without ever knowing the details behind it. But from that time on, this villager was followed by the ghost of the wandering priest, and all around him strange and remarkable things began to happen.

Today the sword is worshipped as the Zaisho-Myōjin [a local Shintō god] idol. And the place where the priest's *juzu* [rosary] and *kesa* [surplice] were found the people call Juzu Valley, or sometimes Kesa Valley. The vengeful ghosts of the wandering priest's family finally turned into bull buffaloes. Even today, dozens of these buffaloes gather together in the mountains there, and with their bellowing, they shake all the mountains and valleys. So they say.[17]

The spirit of hunger, Hidarugami, makes an appearance in a number of legends. The *hidaru* (hunger) *kami* is a devilish, evil spirit, a ghost who can possess anyone who travels in the mountains. Stories about Hidarugami are heard mostly in western Japan, where the two following legends were collected. The word *hidaru* is thought to derive from *darui* (or *hidarui*), "tired" or "exhausted."

According to Japanese folk belief, when someone becomes possessed by this spirit, he suddenly feels very hungry and weak; often he cannot go another step, or he loses consciousness. In the worst cases, he can drop dead on the spot. Sometimes this is because the provisions being carried on the journey have suddenly and mysteriously disappeared. If you encounter this spirit, you should eat something immediately, even if it is only a small morsel, or throw a piece of your own clothing behind you. As a preventive, anyone setting out on a journey or starting a mountain climb should eat until fully stuffed. Or you can lick the written character *kome* (rice) from your hand, or you can throw a part of your provisions into a nearby thicket as an offering.

This spirit appears mostly at crossroads, trails over passes, or caves in the mountains. In some localities, it is believed that Hidarugami also shows up on the sea or at cremations. Possession by Hidarugami is based on the belief that the spirits of people who have died of starvation will seek to haunt living persons, causing them to experience extreme hunger. In many locales, this spirit is identified with a mountain or water deity (Misaki-gami). Misaki-gami was originally an ancestral deity whose abode was the underworld; he or she would help, protect, and lead living descendants in times of emergency.

In this legend, we see the transformation of the originally helpful actions of a deity into destructive or fearsome attributes, indicating that the concept has not remained static—either in time or across the many locales in Japan where it has been encountered by collectors. Incidentally, not only people but also domesticated livestock are subject to Hidarugami possession.

HIDARUGAMI IN THE MOUNTAINS

A man who might have been a pilgrim or a wandering monk was once traveling along the dangerous path over Genmyō Pass, trying to get from Yashiro village to Ankashō city. Those who saw him say he looked very weak, as though he hadn't eaten for a long time. Slowly and with great difficulty, he worked his way up the mountain. That steep, stony path pained him a lot, but finally, using his cane, he reached the pass.

When he looked from the pass and saw the steep path he had to go down, I guess the descent seemed hopeless. The thought must have come to him that it might even be better to die up there and go to hell than climb all the way down that steep path. So he sat down, and he was so weak that he couldn't move anymore.

For a few days, he lay there like that, and finally he died of hunger and exhaustion. Later on, the people found his body, and buried him on the mountain, even though they didn't know who he was. They erected two gravestones for him, too, as a memorial. Eventually, people called these stones "Hidarugami."

In later times, if anyone up in these hills said he was hungry, he suddenly found he couldn't stand up. People still speak about it today. When someone unexpectedly thinks he won't be able to remain standing, he's supposed to give Hidarugami a bite of rice cake. Then a person can stand up and walk along all right. That's what people say about these two memorial stones.[18]

HIDARUGAMI IN TOWN

Once a servant of mine suddenly passed out on the street near Daian-ji Temple—that is, he was possessed by Hidarugami and could hardly talk. Luckily a traveler came along just then, and was able to help my servant and bring him home. It wasn't until he had eaten a piece of *manjū* [a sweet rice and bean cake] that he could speak and tell us what had happened.

An old man who had seen this occurrence was also later suddenly possessed by Hidarugami on the street near the crematorium. This old man told me that he was able to save his life by writing the character for "rice" on the palm of his hand, and then licking it off. He advised me to do the same if I should ever be captured or possessed by Hidarugami.[19]

The dog is the earliest domesticated animal in Japan, with dog graves from the Jōmon era indicating the high value once placed on the animal. In many legends and tales, the dog appears as a hunting companion, a protector, a finder of treasures, a faithful and obedient retainer. The hunter in the next legend not only forgets or overlooks these virtues in his aging and senile dog (as many people do with their elderly human relations), but he also arrogantly loses his temper and strikes out against the dead. He thus gets exactly what he deserves through his own actions. The motif of revenge being carried out by even a small part of a betrayed victim is widespread in Japanese lore.

THE HUNTING DOG'S REVENGE

A hunter who lived near here had a hunting dog for years, but gradually the dog got so old, lame, and tired that he couldn't do what his master wanted. So the hunter got angry at the dog. But the dog growled so that the man knew he would get bitten if he tried to push it too hard. So he decided to kill his dog. He took him way back into the mountains and shot him with his hunting rifle and left him there.

About three years later, though, he got curious about what had happened to his dog's carcass, so he went back up to the place where he had shot it. To his amazement, he found the dog sitting up there, but as just a skeleton, as if he were looking at his master.

This annoyed that hunter so much that he kicked the skeleton aside, and it fell over in a heap. But with this kick, a small sharp bone was driven into the hunter's leg, where it pained him and caused such a bad infection that finally he died from it.[20]

The custom of ringing a bell in a Buddhist temple (by anyone other than a monk summoning others to prayer) is rare, and as far as we can determine is associated mainly with Myōhōsan Temple in Kumano, Wakayama Prefecture, and Zenkō-ji Temple in Nagano Prefecture. Apparently the following legend is based on an older belief that the soul of a recently deceased person will join other local souls on the nearest sacred mountain and slowly change into the collective ancestor deity called *sorei*. Each clan has its own *sorei*, made up of the accumulated souls of people in the group who have died and gone to the other side, where their concern is the welfare and survival of their earthly descendants.

Local mountains remain the focal point of ancestor-complex veneration, and in this narrative, the visit to the temple actualizes the petition of someone who is going to die soon and wants to be assured of life after death. Later the Buddhist use of the temple bell as a call to prayer, or the belief that its sound can reach the ears of Buddha may have played a role in the development of the legend as we now have it. In his *Folk Religion in Japan*, Ichirō Hori devotes an entire chapter to the subject: "Mountains and Their Importance for the Idea of the Other World" (141–79).

While it is common to ring the bell (or to summon the deity by making other loud sounds like clapping) at a Shintō shrine, it is not usual for individuals on their own to perform this act at a Buddhist temple; thus this legend may have grown out of a particular local custom. In any case, the Buddhist temple and its bell would be a part of the normal symbolic setting for death rituals. The story dramatizes the striking, unusual way in which a person "announces" his own death in culturally meaningful imagery.

THE BELL AT MYŌHŌ-SAN TEMPLE

Once a man named Nisaku lived in the village of Hamanakamura in the Amakusa district. At that time, he was about sixty years old. One day, Nisaku was on his way to ring the bell at Myōhō-san Temple. In those days, people felt there was a blessing in it. They believed that they should ring this bell at least once in their lifetime in order to pray for their life after death. If a person was unable to ring the bell during his life, it was thought that he would appear at this temple just after the moment of his death so he could ring the bell while the family members were preparing the funeral dinner. For that reason, the bell was constantly ringing, day and night, all year long. If you didn't see anyone even though the bell was ringing, it meant that some recently deceased person had hurried there in order to ring the bell for himself.

Nisaku was happy that finally before he died he had been able to get to this temple. He rang the bell, prayed for his life after death, and feeling happy about the fulfilling of his wish, headed toward home.

As he climbed down the mountain in the darkening twilight, he suddenly met Jin-san, who lived in the same village. At first, Nisaku was so surprised that he couldn't say anything. Only after he had calmed down a little did he speak to Jin-san. But in the same instant, Jin-san disappeared into the darkness. Nisaku couldn't understand, but finally decided not to dwell on it.

When he finally got back to his home in the village, he learned to his amazement that Jin-san had died in the meanwhile. Shortly before Nisaku had seen him on the mountain, Jin-san had died of a stroke.

Many people say that the recently deceased person goes to the temple dressed in a white funeral shroud in order to ring the bell. Others say that the dead one goes in the everyday clothing that he wore when he died. When Nisaku met Jin-san, he was dressed in everyday clothes with the Kasuri pattern.[21]

Fires appearing in unlikely places like mountainsides or graveyards indicate the presence of ghosts or supernatural beings, and Japanese illustrations of ghosts usually have a couple tongues of flame somewhere in the picture. In places where such lights appear consistently over a long period of time, the phenomenon may have its own local name (the suffix *-hi* or *-bi* means flame).

KECHIBI FOXFIRE IN HOKKEKYŌDŌ

There was a kind of foxfire in Hokkekyōdō, which lies about four kilometers north of the city where Kōchi Castle stands. The people called this flame "Kechibi," and it got to be quite famous. There had been a letter carrier who had lost an important letter somewhere in the pass between Azauno village and Kureno-Shigekura.

His conscience tortured him so much that finally he took his own life. His ghost changed into a death flame and kept searching for the lost letter. So they say.

Later the people buried memorial tablets with Hokke sutras on them, or erected memorial columns in order to calm the ghost of the letter carrier, and they named this spot Hokkekyō Pass. Here in this area, the mysterious flame appeared often, and from a distance you could hardly tell it apart from the torch of a mountain worker. But when the light shone steadily and remained on the mountain without moving, then people knew it was this flame. So they say.

In that area, there was a man named Saburi Jirō. When he was young, one time he and a number of friends went deer hunting in the area around Kurenobe Cliffs. The hunt lasted until nighttime, so the young people came down carrying about twenty or thirty torches. When a few of them said jokingly that death flames couldn't burn with so many flames as their torches, the foxfire appeared around them suddenly in the form of several thousand flames. These shone everywhere on and around the mountains. Then the young men brought their thirty torches together in one place, and immediately the death flame became one huge flame, gigantic as a mountain. As the torches separated again, so the death flame appeared to break into single flames. Several times it happened.

Finally, the people got really scared; they became quiet and climbed silently down the mountain. The flame pursued them all the way to the Mitsuishi neighborhood of Eguchi village. That's what they said. A man named Kusunose Daishi wrote down that he had heard this story directly from Mr. Saburi. The death flame Kechibi is said to come immediately when a person spits on the sole of his straw sandal and says, "Hei, Kechibi!" When I was young, I often heard this story from the older folks.[22]

The Hokke-sutra (Hokkekyō) is especially associated with a particular chapel (-*dō*). Just as the sutra has an impact on the welfare of the dead, so language in general has a power which must be used with care: mentioning the name of this strange fire can actually call it into existence. Of course, the legend is not about the fire, but the fire describes and articulates the guilt of the letter carrier for allowing a piece of mail to go astray; and this in turn bears eloquent testimony to the high regard for compulsive attention to the details of one's job. One is reminded again of the legend of Okiku, who commits suicide over a missing dish, and who, even though she is not guilty, must spend eternity counting the remaining dishes over and over.

The idea of interfamily feuds is common enough in Japanese lore; what distinguishes the next legend is the ironic way in which two highly emotional landowners actually kill themselves through their compulsive argument over a small boundary dispute. The story of course indicates the importance of property to a family's survival. Each tries bitterly not to allow his family's land holdings to become smaller: a real and perennial issue in Japan, where arable land is so limited. The death of a father destabilizes a family; land acquisition stabilizes it. The fanatical involvement of the two wealthy men in their unresolvable and stubborn strife is dramatized by the wrestling ghosts, and strikes many Japanese as more humorous than haunting.

THE TWO WRESTLING GHOSTS

Between the two small places called Hakusui and Kōri in the village of Hanaoka in the Kimotsuki district, there are two grave mounds which lie about ten *chō* [about 3270 ft.] apart. In the old days, two very rich men lived there, one in Kōri, the other in Hakusui. Between their lands lay some very beautiful rice fields which the two wrangled about constantly, because each one wanted to own them. Although they had argued a long time, they had never been able to come to an agreement, so finally they settled matters by making each other a promise: whichever one of them could commit suicide first by slitting his belly open on an appointed day of a particular month at the stroke of a certain temple bell would take over ownership of these fields.

At the appointed stroke of the clock, the rich man of Hakusui slit his belly open and died. But the rich man of Kōri had killed himself first, and so the disputed fields came into his possession and became his property.

So the ghost of the rich man from Hakusui couldn't find any peace of mind, and when it rained in the night, he came out of his grave and flew back and forth over these fields. The other ghost, the rich man from Kōri, then came out of his grave and also flew there to protect his rice fields against his rival. Finally, the ghosts ran at each other, they say, and wrestled.[23]

Omens

Fate or destiny appears in Japanese legends, as it does throughout Japanese folk belief, as a power exercised by the gods. Humans are seldom able to escape their fate, and many legends attest to the certainty with which foreordained events take place even when knowledgeable people try to avoid them. That the gods can occasionally be outwitted or circumvented is illustrated by a smaller number of stories. Yanagita discusses three common types of destiny legends in *The Yanagita Kunio Guide to the Japanese Folk Tale* (1986, 192–96).

Beyond acting as stories which dramatize broadly accepted ideas about fate, such legends may also be ways of speculating about the possibility that some people may possess special capabilities for parapsychological experience. Belief in clairvoyance is strong in Japan (see "The Aunt's Dream"), and—as is the case in other cultures—legends can illustrate or rationalize experiences outside the realm of normal, everyday life.

A BRIDE RESCUED FROM HER FATE

One time two fishermen were sleeping out on the beach. One of them lay awake in the night, and he suddenly heard two gods speaking to each other. They were saying that in both neighboring towns the birth of a child was expected soon. He eavesdropped on their conversation very attentively. They were considering what kind of fate they wanted to prescribe for the two expected children. The fisherman began to realize that the gods who were speaking were the gods of fate—the ones who decide good and bad luck for human lives.

The one god said, "I'll give the boy luck," and the other said, "I'll give the girl an unlucky life." "We'll let them marry each other," they decided, "and when the wedding procession starts out for the man's village, we'll send a heavy rain. The bride will try to find shelter from the weather in a hollow tree, but we'll have the storm break up the tree, and the tree will fall on the girl and kill her."

When the fisherman heard all this, he was deeply shocked, because he knew only one woman in his village who was supposed to have a baby in the near future. It couldn't be anyone else: it must be the wife of his friend, the other fisherman.

Now, when the child had actually come into the world, the fisherman felt his fear and consternation come back, especially when he saw that the child was in fact a girl. But he didn't dare give away the secret, or he would have brought down the heaviest anger of the gods on himself. Gradually, though, he lost his anxiety and finally forgot the girl and what he had heard that night.

But when the girl turned twenty-one and was to marry a boy of the same age from the neighboring village, he remembered the gods' conversation he had overheard. He went along with the wedding procession. As they got about halfway to the other village, the group was surprised by a violent rain and thunderstorm. And, sure enough, there by the side of the path was a big, hollow tree where the bride was able to get out of the storm. But this fisherman remembered the plans of the fate gods, and was afraid that the tree might fall and kill the bride if it was uprooted by the storm. So, even though the others were shocked when he did it, he yanked the bride out and away from the tree.

They had hardly gotten out of reach when a bolt of lightning struck the tree and it collapsed. But the bride was safe and sound. So everybody thanked the fisherman, and finally he was able to tell them about what he had overheard that night on the shore twenty-one years earlier.[24]

In many western Märchen, the device of interdiction/ interdiction-violated allows a complication to take place which is then brought to a resolution by the rest of the story. In the next legend, violating the interdiction is a normal result of the father's concern for the life of his son. But since the gods of fate have ordained how the son will die, it is almost immaterial whether the father intentionally breaks the interdiction or does it by accident or simply waits for a knife to fall on his son. In this case, it may be ironic that the son indeed helps to carry out his own fate, but the basic idea is that he cannot avoid it anyhow.

THE YOUNG MAN AND THE CARVING KNIFE

A traveling merchant was staying overnight in a chapel along the road one time, and as he was lying awake in the night, he overheard the gods of fate talking to each other. They were talking about his own son, and they were planning his fate. He had decided to go into architecture, and they were planning how he would die at work by means of a carving knife when he got to be twenty years old.

Later, when the son gradually grew up and reached this dangerous age, his father kept him from doing any work with such tools. But in spite of his father's orders, the son worked at woodcutting, and one day he wounded himself so badly that he died of it. That's what they say.[25]

Mushrooms are prominent in Japanese folklore, often appearing as spirits transformed into dancing or singing beings who seduce the unwary traveler or threaten to kill him. In a story called "The Man-eating Mushroom," a mushroom says, "When I call to men, it is strange how one after another drops dead" (Mayer 1984, 128–30).

Because of the ubiquitous appearance of mushrooms in stories and beliefs about death, we may assume that even so brief a legend as the one which follows triggers many complicated, but related, associations in the minds of its listeners. In the dramatic sense, the meaning is symbolically clear even without any traditional implications: a plant which springs from dying materials is discovered flourishing in the hearth, center of the family's life. The fact that the mushroom is remarkable or strange, even unrecognizable, enhances its extraordinary possibilities for meaning. Just as humans are expected to act like everyone else, so phenomena of nature are supposed to conform to norms. Thus anything abnormal registers as negative; on the level of everyday occurrences, anything out of place is potentially dangerous. Whenever a strange plant appears in a garden without having been planted, it is seen as a sign of impending disaster. This is especially true of the *higan* (solstice)-*bana* (flower), a red flower that blooms in autumn. When bamboo suddenly blooms, there is the same assumption of bad luck or disaster brewing.

The form of a ghost suggested by a mysterious moon hovering over a weeping willow by the water. Artist: Kōson (other information unknown).

A friend of the authors, a woman from Osaka, tells that her aunt married a very rich man and led a luxurious life until one day in September, when the whole yard suddenly bloomed with *higan-bana.* Even the gardener could not tell where the flowers had come from and was very puzzled. Not long afterward, the husband lost his business and eventually died, and the aunt had to seek refuge with her sister's family. The family still identifies the plant as the omen of disaster.

MUSHROOMS AS OMENS OF DEATH

There was a mother who lived near here with her son. He had a job, so every day he left home and went to work. One day after he had gone, she decided to build a fire, so she pushed the ashes in the fireplace over to one side. But there in the space she had cleared, she discovered a strange mushroom that she didn't recognize. As soon as she saw it, she felt frightened, but she didn't know why.

That evening she waited as she always did for her son to come home from work. But he didn't arrive. She got the news later that he had been killed by an accident on the job.

They say that a family which eats such a mushroom will die out right away, and those who find one in their garden will begin to get poor. Eventually they'll become totally impoverished.[26]

Omens are taken seriously in Japanese tradition, whether they assume the form of dreams, visions, or hallucinatory episodes. Through the 1930s, it was widely believed in some areas (for example, on the island of Ōshima) that the sight of a phantom funeral procession with torches presaged a local death. The psychological dimension of this reaction has not been much investigated, so we cannot speculate with confidence about whether the idea reflects community "psychic" sensitivity to traumatic events translated into visual terms, or whether the legends constitute rationalizations of strange or unrecognized phenomena (like swamp gas, phosphorescent wood, nightmares, and the like). Often, because we assume the latter explanation is the most "logical," we hesitate to consider other possibilities, and the result is that we do not develop a fuller view which might account for the longevity and consistency of the legends and their cultural interpretations. The following three legends are typical.

AUDIBLE DEATH OMENS

The following story was told to me by my father. It concerns something which took place shortly before the death of his grandmother. It was in year twenty-eight of the Meiji era [1896], and my father was twenty-four years old when it happened.

"One evening," he said to me, "when I came through the courtyard of the house as I usually did, I heard someone over by the storage shed pounding nails into a board. I thought that was strange, so I got to wondering about it, and finally went over where the hammering was going on to ask what it was. Your grandfather answered and said he wasn't doing anything; he wondered why I had asked. So I told him about the noise I had just heard. We couldn't figure it out, so eventually we forgot about it.

"About ten days later, on the day of the Urabon Festival, my grandmother fell ill and died within two days. Her death was sudden, completely unexpected. Because of that, we didn't have a chance to prepare very well for the funeral. So we had to make the coffin out of a big wooden box. It got built exactly on the same spot where I had earlier heard that mysterious sound of nailing—which was exactly like the noise of constructing Grandmother's coffin.

"Two or three days after I had heard that sound of hammering by the storehouse, the whole family was sitting around together chatting after a meal. Suddenly we heard something hit the ground, as if something heavy had been thrown into the front garden. My father asked who was there, stood up, and looked out into the garden. But he didn't see anyone, nor any trace of anything that someone might have thrown. So eventually we forgot about it. But this noise that the whole family heard was exactly like the impact of the rice sacks that were thrown down into the garden from the rice storage shed when they prepared the funeral dinner to honor my dead grandmother."[27]

THE AUNT'S DREAM

About thirty-five years ago, when I was a schoolboy in Takagi, I used to stop and visit my aunt on the way home from school. One day when I was there, she suddenly asked me if anyone in my own village had recently died. Well, I didn't know of anybody. So she asked me if anyone there had been ill lately. But I hadn't heard of anyone falling sick, either.

She said that very soon there would be a death in some family in my village. In fact, just that noon she had seen someone digging in the Akagina cemetery, right there where the dead of the Akagi family were buried. For that reason, it couldn't be anyone other than a person of that family. She very clearly told me the name of the person who was going to die, and she even named the gravediggers, three of them, she had seen. It made me feel really strange, because I knew that my aunt was supposed to be clairvoyant. People in the family thought she had this supernatural ability to see into the future.

I stayed overnight with her that time, and the next morning, I went with her to the place where she had seen the gravediggers at work. But there was no trace of anyone, no sign that anyone had been doing any digging.

I went home and told my family about it. About a week later, the head of the family my aunt had spoken about suddenly took sick and died after four or five days. Since the ancestors of this family had been Akagis, he was buried in the Akagi plot in the graveyard. To bury him, they hired three gravediggers, exactly the ones my aunt had named a week before.[28]

A DROWNING OMEN

Toward the end of the Meiji emperor's rule [about 1910], there lived in Teibu in the village of Kasari a man named Tokutaro. He had been a lifelong servant of Lord Shigenobu Yaohachi, and he was very stupid. Sometime about the fortieth year of the Meiji Period, on the same day that Tokutaro's wife drowned, someone was going around that morning saying that a person had drowned in the river. The whole village was astonished, and everyone rushed down to where the drowning was supposed to have happened, and they searched for the corpse. Tokutaro's wife was also there. After looking around the place, they finally decided that no one could have drowned, so they all forgot about it and went home.

Two or three hours later, Tokutaro's wife and her five-year-old daughter went to a pool along the riverbank to wash vegetables. As she worked, some of the vegetables drifted away from her in the wind, and when she tried to grab them, she fell into the water. She was pregnant, and that made her very clumsy, and so she couldn't climb back up the bank. So finally she drowned.

The child yelled to her, but it didn't do any good, so she ran back to the village and got help. Of course, when the people came to the pool, there was nothing they could do but pull the corpse onto the shore. The villagers talked about it for a long time, and they wondered if the rumor they had heard that morning wasn't some kind of omen of this woman's death.[29]

Ghosts at Sea

According to coastal Japanese folk belief, the spirits of people who have died in sea disasters can appear in ghostly ships on the sea. Usually the phantom ship materializes suddenly during a jet black night, in thick fog, or sometimes by moonlight. The ghosts on board often demand that a ladle or bucket be passed to them, but careful Japanese fishermen and seafaring people know that you must supply only a bucket without a bottom; otherwise the ghosts will use it to fill your ship with water until it sinks. The subjects of such encounters need not be guilty of any particular offense against the dead, but are simply victims of the residual *goryō* of unburied and unritualized people who have died at sea. In Japanese folk belief, the *funa yūrei* (ghost ship) is believed to be an actual phenomenon which can be seen—as compared with many other ghostly occurrences which are only heard or felt.

The term *funa yūrei* is a collective expression designating the ghost ship itself as well as other ghosts on the phantom ship or in the sea (see "Ghost Heads in the Water"). Konno Ensuke suggests that the concept is based on someone having seen a real derelict ship, perhaps filled with skeletal remains; but whether the idea has such a concrete foundation or not, it certainly reflects the intense Japanese concern that the dead can be dangerous and affect one's welfare; the dead can make demands, and these demands must be met, albeit with care (what the ghosts demand from the living varies in different regions of Japan).

The image is similar to the Flying Dutchman, where the whole ship, along with its crew, is considered a phantom—one which can cause real damage or death to the live sailors who encounter it. Other spirits, such as the heads floating in the water in one legend, are not necessarily connected to a particular ship and are more likely local *yūrei*. These legends cluster around the areas where Japanese coastal waters have long demonstrated their danger and fickleness: straits where currents run strong or reverse directions during changes in the tides, areas where whirlpools are likely to appear, and spots where rocks, sand spits, and reefs continually imperil those who make their living on the sea.

But while the legends may incorporate real considerations about safety, the story is most often a dramatic reminder that seafarers owe their survival not only to skill, but to their relationship with the values of their village and occupational group—which includes obligations to sailors who have already died. To ignore tradition is foolhardy; to anger the dead by not providing for them tempts fate; to be in a place where others have died subjects you to forces beyond your control. Avoidance, care, ritual, respect, tradition: these are the bywords. On occasion, proper behavior may elicit more constructive reactions from the dead: in a few legends, the spirits of those who died by water have warned or saved ships in danger. But a sailor would be wise not to count on it.

Not surprisingly, Obon is the most common time of year for the appearance of *funa yūrei*. Since this festival celebrates dead souls, the appearance of ghost ships at this time is appropriate, but it also indicates that anyone who sets sail during that season is foolhardy or ignorant of tradition (compare the continued unwillingness of commercial fishermen in the United States to leave port on a Friday). The belief may have a practical purpose as well: when people are told not to go fishing during Obon Festival, it may show that the fishermen have planned a regular rest period which coincides with ritual activity.

Some say that to distinguish a ghost ship from a real one, a person should bend over and look upside down between his or her own legs at the vessel. If it appears to be floating directly on the water, then it is a real ship; if, however, it appears to be floating in the air, it is a ghost ship. In

The Hokusai Sketch-Books (1958, 138), Michener includes a print called *Ship Ghosts* by Hokusai (1760–1849), accompanied by an explanatory note on the well-known attempt by ghosts to fill up a boat with ladles full of water. The ghost ship legends presented here came mostly from central and northern Japan, where the coastal waters are particularly dangerous.

GHOSTS IN THE SEA

Sometimes when a ship travels along the coast west of Onigasaki village (in the Ise country), it will suddenly be unable to move if it lowers its sail. At the Konpira Shrine, which stands nearby on the shore, hang many votive pictures in which you can see painted scenes of seafarers in distress, sailors kneeling with their caps off and their hands folded in prayer, looking toward heaven for a message that flutters down to them from the gods. Once a man named Yashichi went fishing there on the sixteenth day of the Bon Festival and never came back. That's how dangerous the place is.

Ships that pass there at night often notice that something touches their rudder. In the next instant, they see a blue fireball rolling over the waves like a ghostly missile, and this turns into something that looks like a giant ladle. The sailors get panicked, and they think that this ladle is holding onto their boat; they go into a kind of shock.

Around this area, they also tell about how along Cape Kamagasaki [near Osaka] the fishermen catch sardines after mid-October. At this time, the whole beach is alive with people fishing. The people fish between two o'-clock in the afternoon and nine in the evening, which means that there is time for them to throw out their nets at least twice. But on the third and fourth day of the month by the old calendar (that is, toward the beginning of November), the fishermen don't believe in throwing out any nets at all. If they do, as they pull their nets in, their boat is surrounded secretly underwater by naked men with ladles in their hands who circle the boat. They sing sad and reproachful songs, and with these ladles they fill the boat so quickly with water that it goes down. Then the strange men cry, "Come along with us! Come along with us!" and vanish in the sea. This is supposed to mean that those who have drowned in the sea near this spot are calling for more comrades. So they say.

On the nights after these happenings, seafarers who travel by the cape hear mourning voices from the bottom of the sea. These voices call repeatedly, begging for help. Any fishermen who hear these voices are deeply shocked. If you hear these voices three times, you'll see a bright blue fireball near the ship, as big as a washtub. It flashes a few times, then disappears. Anyone who sees this light several times gets dizzy and falls unconscious. If you saw it right in front of your face, you would immediately pass out. Finally, all the sailors on board get dizzy and suffer the whole night. This also comes from the spirits of drowned people, so they say.[30]

GHOST HEADS IN THE WATER

The old fishermen around here have a story about trying to come back into port with the catch, but their boat seems to get caught and can't move through the water. In spite of good winds and powerful men at the oars, the land just doesn't come any closer.

There, floating in the water, the fishermen see skulls biting at their oars. The more experienced ones know immediately, even in the dead of night, that these skulls are from sailors who have drowned at sea. They then read a Buddhist text, wrap themselves up in their blankets, and lie down to sleep. When they awake, they find the heads have vanished, and then when they begin to row, they can easily reach port.

Young, inexperienced fishermen, though, often think they have to act brave, and they try to hit these skulls with their oars, and they row as hard as they can to reach shore. But they have to pay a price for this. Their families get nighttime death premonitions the next time their men go out, and afterward, in spite of good sailing weather, the fishermen never come back. The skulls take their revenge for being hit with the oars.

Even if only one young man tries to hit the skulls, when that ship sets sail next time, the whole crew will go down: father, brother, and sons.[31]

THE GHOST SHIP

Often it happens that fishermen catch sight of a big sailing ship at night, or in the fog—sometimes with shimmering blue human figures on board who call out. If their call is a strange one—a signal that the fishermen don't understand—then they believe they shouldn't answer it. If they do respond, they believe they'll be seized by a panic that the other ship will ram them and run them under.

They go out of their heads and maneuver their boat so crazily that a serious accident really happens to them.[32]

GHOST SHIPS AND SHIP GHOSTS

In Kanegasaki in Chikuzen Province, the fishermen don't go out to fish on the thirteenth and fifteenth days of the month during Obon season. If you go out fishing in spite of this belief, they say, you will be met by a ghost ship. And really what happens is that the ship ghost stretches out its white hands and hangs down from the upper deck. When that happens, you're supposed to light the end of a broom and sweep the deck with it. Then the ghost will vanish. For that reason, a big ship is always outfitted with a broom.

The phenomenon of the ocean surface turning completely white at night is called *shiki-yūrei*. If you sail into it, your ship suddenly loses its power to move. Then the helmsman should give the spirit a ladle, so they say.

The fishermen also raised beans that were thrown around at the festival on the seventh day of the first month on the old calendar, Shōgatsu. Only after they had put some of these beans in their sea chests would they go out fishing. And when a sudden storm or fog sprang up and put them in danger, they'd throw these beans into the water. That's what they say.[33]

THE SHIPWRECK AT SETO

At the time of the Meiji Restoration [after 1868], a fishing boat got caught in a terrible storm off Seto, where many ships had already been wrecked. The captain and his men had to fight a life and death struggle against the storm in order to avoid a wreck, and they were trying to reach their home port as fast as they could. The ship was not really far from port when they heard a crashing and screaming, as if they had collided with another boat. But they couldn't do anything about it because they had to work with all their power to bail the water out of their own ship, which was swamped by bigger and bigger waves.

Just then a human head surfaced on the water, and a man grabbed at the gunwales with his hands, held fast, and yelled for help. But no one could help him. As his cries got more desperate, the captain became so rattled that he knocked the man under with an oar. He sank and never came up again.

Afterward people said that in this place a strange light or a flying ghost was seen. The captain who knocked the drowning sailor under during that storm developed such a fear that he gave up his work. But he had to make a living, so he went to work with the mussel fishermen. At that time, another man who had dived deep into the sea looking for mussels found a corpse lying on the ocean floor, clutching a rock. He didn't tell anybody about it for a while.

One day, when the captain was out with the other divers, the sea was full of more fish and mussels than usual. He forgot about his fear of the ocean, and dove in himself. He didn't give any signal to those waiting for him above, and he didn't come up for a long time. So his friends searched for him, but the ocean current was flowing too fast for them to find him right away. Finally, they found him all right, dead and clutching a rock on the sea floor, lying just as his friend had seen that other corpse earlier. After the death of the captain, people didn't see that strange light anymore.[34]

Passions

In the following legend, the *yūrei* is frustrated by the fact that she died with her impossible passion unfulfilled. The situation is further complicated by her vanity, the religious setting, and the selfishness of her uncontrollable love for the priest. Flames in cemeteries are called *hitodama* and are considered to be the ignited spirits of dead persons, a concept so commonly understood in Japanese lore that a red or blue flame appearing in the corner of a block print or the setting of a legend is enough to assure the viewer or listener that death or *yūrei* are involved. In traditional anecdotes, the flames are seen just before someone dies and later are interpreted as an omen.

Umibozu, a sea-phantom who appears suddenly and darkens the sky. Artist: Hōen (other information unknown).

THE GHOST OF THE TEMPLE MAIDEN

We used to hear this story back in the 1930s in the neighborhood of Iōji Temple in Aichi Prefecture. There is still a temple there called Dōrinji in the Imaoka area of today's village of Fujimatsu, which lies about four kilometers north of Iōji. At one time, a maid worked at this Dōrinji Temple. She was efficient and good, but she had an ugly face.

Later this maid came to Iōji Temple to work there. The priest was a very handsome man, and the girl soon fell in love with him. She wanted to please him, and she did everything she could think of to attract his attention. But the priest only served Buddha, only thought about Buddha. Besides that, the maid was too ugly for him.

But she couldn't get rid of her passion, and she just loved the priest more and more emotionally. She crept silently into the temple every night, and secretly took a little oil out of the lamp which stood next to the Buddha statue, and used it on her hair to make it shiny and beautiful. The priest noticed it before long and scolded her violently, and drove her out of the temple forever. Because of her grief and pain over her unrequited love for the priest, she soon killed herself.

The priest from Dōrinji Temple, where the maid had previously served, had pity on her, and laid her to rest in the burial ground of his temple, and read sutras for her. But after the burial, especially when it was really dark and rainy, people began seeing every night a small, blue light rising like a candle from the grave of this maiden. Then it would flutter along the bank of the river to Iōji Temple.

There was a local young man who wanted to see this light for himself, so on one dark rainy night, he hid himself behind the embankment of the river and waited for the spirit to come by. A blue light really appeared over the grave of the maiden, he said, and came closer and closer along with a really sinister-sounding wind. The boy still waited, and held his breath. The light kept coming closer, and hovered just so high over the ground as if somebody carried it by hand. The boy saw no human figure, nothing other than the blue light, which made a sputtering noise like burning oil. It sounded as though someone kept whispering: "How annoying! How annoying!" It was extremely eerie for him, and he cried out before he realized it. Then the light suddenly retreated in the direction it had come from.

So said the young man anyway. People said they saw this appearance of lights up until the beginning of the Meiji era. But the dead girl has long since found her rest, and this story has become just an old legend. In those days, though, people said that this light might be the spirit of the dead girl, who kept coming back after her death—restless and unredeemed—passionately sad about her unfulfilled love and punished for her theft of the holy oil from the temple. Her spirit wandered the four kilometers every night from the grave to this temple in order to see her beloved priest, and to ask forgiveness from Buddha for the stolen oil.[35]

One of the most widely known of Japanese *yūrei* legends is "Botandōrō" (The peony lantern); it is believed to have taken place in the Nezu district of Tokyo, the neighborhood in which the Zenshōan Temple is located, and it became the basis for a popular Rakugo presentation composed in 1884 by Enchō Sanyūtei, the famous storyteller who ended his days at Zenshōan and whose private collection of ghost pictures is now guarded and annually shown in that temple. There are many versions of the story, one of which was published in 1899 by Lafcadio Hearn under the title "A Passional Karma" in the collection *In Ghostly Japan*. In the legend, a young student named Saburō falls in love with a beautiful young woman, Otsuyu, the daughter of his father's best friend. They meet secretly and agree that eventually they will be married. But Saburō becomes ill, and the couple do not see each other for a long time.

When Saburō later goes to visit Otsuyu, he is told she (and her maid) have died. He prays for her soul during the Obon Festival (not surprisingly, it is the anniversary of their meeting); while he is in the cemetery praying, he hears the sound of approaching footsteps, and notices two women who look remarkably like Otsuyu and her maid. It turns out that it is indeed Otsuyu, and their excited conversation soon reveals that her aunt—who is opposed to their relationship—has circulated the rumor about Otsuyu's death, and has also told her that Saburō has died. The two, now reunited but frightened about being discovered, decide to meet secretly. Each night, accompanied by the maid carrying an old-fashioned lantern decorated with peonies, Otsuyu stays with Saburō and the maid keeps watch.

But Saburō's servant notices the visits, and in a scene familiar in woodblock prints, he peeks through a hole in the *shōji* panel and sees his employer making passionate love to a decaying skeleton while another skeleton sits in the doorway holding a lantern. He reports this to the local Buddhist priest, who then sets about proving to Saburō that the woman he thinks he's making love to is in fact a *yūrei*. When the priest, the servant, and Saburō finally locate the grave markers of Otsuyu and her maid in a nearby cemetery, Saburō is convinced, and allows himself and his house to be plastered with charms and paper amulets; by staying indoors and praying the Nenbutsu, he is able to ward off the two women's spirits, but slowly his health begins to deteriorate, and his servant begins to worry that his master will die and leave him unemployed if he doesn't have the pleasure of meeting his old love.

So the servant secretly takes the *ofuda* off the door, the ghostly women enter that night, and Saburō and Otsuyu make love again. In the morning, the servant finds Saburō dead, entwined in the arms of a skeleton and his face radiant with tranquility. In such a legend, passion has the power to reach beyond death, and the returning *yūrei*—who died in passionate frustration—exercises love, not revenge, as the dramatic enactment of eternal bonds.[36]

The following three stories focus particularly on love and the ways that the *yūrei* can affect the surviving partner. In "The Spirit of a Loving Bondwoman," the girl's love relation with the young man is unbroken by death in much the same way as the mother-child relationship in other stories. The young girl's family was so poor that she was "sold" into servitude; such arrangements were common in Okinawa, but probably not since the Meiji era. In some cases, the family, or the young woman herself, could earn freedom by repaying the original sum of money. Here one irony is that the girl, despite her poverty and dependency on the rich man, demonstrates a higher set of values than her "owner."

The *jitō* (district governor) in "The Priest, His Niece, and the Jitō" covets a young girl and breaks all the normal procedural rules to obtain her as a second wife. The ghostly fires (foxfire, will-o'-the wisp), the working out of the priest's curse, and the suicide of the young girl are all typical elements of the *yūrei*'s revenge. In keeping with the Japanese

A woman's ghost appears in mosquito netting (many believe that this is the ghost of Otsuyu in the Botandōrō story). Artist: Hiresaki Eimei (other information unknown).

concept of the family (rather than the individual) as the basic social unit, it is the entire family of the *jitō* which suffers, implying that a person's actions and responsibilities are inseparable from the interests and welfare of others. In addition, even the fishermen in the vicinity feel they are in danger from the vengeful spirit of the priest until they dispose of the *jitō's* gravestone (and that of his son as well) in the river. That the bloody footprints of the niece can still be seen is a motif that parallels the votive pictures and other visual tokens in other legends: even though the present audience did not witness the event, there is colorful proof that it did indeed happen.

In another version of "Kiyo and Anchin," a young pilgrim named Anchin asks for overnight lodging in the house of a man called Shōji Kiyotsugu. His daughter, Kiyohime, falls in love with the pilgrim and steals secretly into his room that night in hopes of making love. Anchin refuses, not wanting to do anything unchaste during his pilgrimage. He promises to visit her on his way back from the shrine of Kumano. She waits for several days until she learns from another pilgrim that Anchin has gone home by another route. In a frenzy, she dies, and her spirit pursues Anchin in the form of a dragon. Anchin sees the dragon coming and takes refuge at Dōjō-ji Temple, where the monks hide him under a large bell. The dragon (Kiyohime's vengeful ghost) wraps itself around the bell and strikes it vehemently with its tail until sparks fly, and Anchin is incinerated.

The bell, of course, can still be seen at the temple, and bells of the same type are memorialized on the wooden *ema* (votive pictures) which one can buy there. According to Paul Radin, the Anchin and Kiyo legend was among the most popular of the traditional narratives told by Japanese immigrants to the United States; in the 1940s more than 50 percent of the Japanese-Americans polled in his survey reported knowing the story (1946, 298).

THE SPIRIT OF A LOVING BONDWOMAN

There was a good-looking young civil servant in Okinawa who fell in love with a beautiful young bondwoman. But her owner, who was a very rich man, craved her and wanted to have sex with her. The girl was only interested in the love of that handsome young man, though, and every night they met secretly in the rich man's garden. She was afraid of her owner, so she kept resisting his attempts to get close.

One day, though, he just raped her, right there in his house. Of course, for her that was an unbearable shame, so she killed herself. Even after that, the two lovers kept meeting every night in their special place in the garden. But the young man could see that she was deeply depressed about something.

He finally decided to go to the rich man directly and find out what was going on. That's when he learned that she was already dead, and had been those last times when he had held her so sadly in his arms.[37]

THE PRIEST, HIS NIECE, AND THE *JITŌ*

In the early 1600s, a priest named Eizon from Chōshū set out for Ishinomaki in order to rebuild the Zen Buddhist temple there. He took along his young niece, a beautiful and well-behaved girl. The local *jitō*, Sasamachi Shinzaemon, who was at that time sovereign of the city of Minatomachi, fell in love with this girl, even though he was already married and had a daughter-in-law. He demanded to have the priest's niece as his second wife. The priest refused of course, and it brought down on him the wrath and resentment of the *jitō*, who considered himself a powerful man.

Later on, a controversy developed between the priest and the *jitō* over the boundary line between their lands. The *jitō* brought legal suit against the priest at the civil office which had jurisdiction over the temple area, and collected signatures among people he had been stirring up against the priest. He accused him of having a secret love affair with his niece and was able to maneuver things so that the priest was banished to an island named Enoshima. The priest was so outraged that he placed a curse on the *jitō* and his family, and because of his grief, he refused to eat, so that soon afterward he died. Immediately after his banishment, his niece was brought into the *jitō's* house by force, but she quickly took her own life with a dagger rather than fall into his hands.

From that time onward, people could see a strange light every night on the small mountain behind the *jitō's* house. When the *jitō* himself went outside to see it, he caught sight of the priest up on the mountain hanging upside down from a tree and looking at him with a terribly fierce expression. In his fear, the *jitō* lost his mind and died soon afterward. His son, his daughter-in-law, and all his remaining family members died shortly after that, all of them from unnatural causes, so that his entire family came to an end. Also his successor had no luck in the house, either, and soon received a disciplinary transfer.

The fishermen who lived on the island of Enoshima—where the priest had been banished and where he had died—were afraid of his vengeful spirit. So they took the gravestone of the *jitō* and also the memorial stone of his son from the cemetery of Jiō-in Temple and threw them into the Kitakami River. People say that in that temple you can still see the bloody footprints of the priest's niece.[38]

KIYO AND ANCHIN

At one time, there was a monastery in the village of Minomae in the Shiba district. A monk named Anchin was in his novitiate there, and was once summoned to the village of Goshō in the Iwate district to pray for a rich family by the name of Aniwa. As soon as Kiyo, the daughter of this family, saw Anchin, she fell in love with him because he was so handsome. She confessed her love to him and pursued him obstinately, trying to visit him secretly at night. Finally, Anchin couldn't refuse her any longer, and so he began a love affair with her. But soon he feared that word of it might reach the ears of others in the family, so he quietly left the house.

Kiyo followed him. But when she finally reached the port on the Shizukuishi River, Anchin had already left on a boat. She started weeping over his rejection of her and finally got so depressed that she jumped into a pond near the river and drowned.

Not realizing what had happened, Anchin kept on traveling. On his way from Mii Temple to Negoro Temple, he stayed overnight at Dōjō-ji Temple in the Kii country. During the night, the angry ghost of Kiyo appeared and tortured and tormented him, so that he went crazy and finally died there. That's what people say about Anchin and Kiyo around Shiba.[39]

Epilogue

People indeed say that it happened to Kiyo and Anchin, and they "say" it in a number of ways: in art, in song, in local legend (the way people account for the bell, which is still there), and on *ema*—the small wooden placards sold at shrines to communicate prayers and wishes to the deities. What makes the legend narratives special, of course, is their capacity to dramatize in living speech those cultural abstractions which otherwise remain unarticulated. These stories are not merely entertaining accounts which *mention* or *reference* important cultural values; although entertainment is an important part of any interesting story, legends and other folk narratives allow—even require—the dramatization, and thus the reexperiencing, of culturally based feelings, anxieties, fears, and concerns. Vicarious it may well be, but it is experience nonetheless, and the lifetime accumulation of such experiences confirms and strengthens the values which make sensible and "normal" the everyday world in which we live.

Moreover, as these stories illustrate, not *every* cultural idea achieves articulation in a dramatic legend: there is a selection, and through the years a distillation and intensification, of certain key concepts which have endured in vernacular Japanese culture. The stories in this collection seem to be *about* death and ghosts, but actually the framework of death acts as a stage on which other cultural elements are "brought to life" and made palpable. Prominent among them are the bonds between family members, especially those linking mother and child; the bonds between lovers, between the living and the dead, between humans and their environment, between people and their deities. Indeed the sets of interactive responsibilities thought—ideally at least—to animate most of Japan's vernacular culture and motivate much of its social activity attain living form in these legends.

Whether one believes in ghosts or not, whether one is a practicing Buddhist or not, whether one can knowledgeably list the abstract values of Japanese culture or not is quite beside the point. The legends are still told because they embody values which are functional, recognizable, experiential in the vernacular field of reference—or else they would mean nothing to those who tell and hear them.

Nothing testifies so eloquently to the perseverance of these ideas in the popular culture of Japan as the continual proliferation of films, comics, cartoons, and popular novels featuring ghosts and death, which reveal the same—obviously untired—shared anxieties about interpersonal obligations dramatized in the folk legends. Nothing verifies the endurance of these long-standing ideas in everyday life as vividly as the modern versions of these legends being told by worldly wise taxi drivers in worldly wise Tokyo. And nothing illustrates the cultural gulf between the vernacular and elite levels in contemporary Japan more concretely than Emperor Hirohito's recent funeral: virtually nothing mentioned in this book was to be seen. His was a formal, imperial, Shintō funeral different in practically every way from the vernacular Buddhist funerals which were probably taking place among his subjects at the same time. Families in Japan now often videotape their funerals (as they do their weddings), and it is these homemade videos, not an imperial news release, that embody the rituals and beliefs which give ongoing substance and depth to stories like the ones in this brief collection.

And why should this not be so? For all its rapprochement with the Western world (which was earlier viewed as a signal of Japanese enlightenment, and is now perceived by some as a sign of international aggression), Japan's cultural factors remain unchanged; it is still a country where sharply divergent individualism is discouraged, and family ties, sealed with all manner of obligation, responsibility, and even guilt, create the weft upon which everyday culture is woven. From the first arrivals in Japan of businessmen and missionaries (who for different reasons promoted the idea of separable individualism) and especially since the social changes of the Meiji era, these concepts of family interdependency have been put under considerable stress. Perhaps this is why the legends have thrived, for they dramatize the anxieties felt by many people about what will happen to their children, and they act out uncertainty about life and death, fear of betrayal in a culture based on obligation, concern for beauty in a changing world, worries about land and livelihood in a crowded and competitive country, all the ambiguities felt by families in modern times.

A culture facing fearsome questions with no easy answers provides a reservoir of opportunity for legend narrators; the apparent factuality, the localization, the sense of verifiability all conspire to lend a feeling of certainty, while the story itself usually dances along a borderline between the usual and the unusual, the familiar and the scary, the acceptable and the frightful. The intersection between the living and the dead, especially in a culture where the land of the dead has interacted so actively in the world of the living, offers a fertile field for metaphor and suggestion in stories which hinge on fear, uncertainty, and anxiety. As Jan H. Brunvand has pointed out, American contemporary legends, viewed thematically, dramatize the very abstractions that bother Americans or make them most anxious: sex, age, death, dating, marriage, religion, travel abroad, eating away from home. The same can be said of Japanese legends.

Thus a close look at the legends provides us with a wonderfully sensitive barometer of deeply set Japanese values. This reading cannot be used to devise a stereotype, however, for not every Japanese person will register or express these ideas in the same way. These stories indicate tendencies, attitudes, generalized feelings; they do not generate a specific list of rules on how to live in Japanese society. But, unless we insist that these stories have been passed along out of pure, old-fashioned hardheadedness and blind ignorance, we must conclude that they do reveal a range of real concerns and recognizable cultural values.

For this reason, we feel that the aggregate voice represented here speaks louder and clearer than the isolated voice of one individual. Vernacular expression is significant not only because it represents the shared views of the otherwise-overlooked, everyday crowd but because—in cultural terms—it is more articulate than any single individual, and longer lasting. We believe that the Japanese people, who have kept these legends alive through the years, will agree with us. Their ghosts are the wellsprings for distilled dramatizations and cameos of the cultural values and experiences that animate their society.

Sources and Notes

1. "Kasamatsu Pass and Turtle Rock." Source: Hirata Yoshimitsu, "Rikuzen Asahiura ni Densetsu o tazunete," *Tabi to Densetsu* 4, no. 2 (1931): 73.

2. "A Weeping Stone." Source: Mori Mashio, "Sai no Yonakiishi," *Tabi to Densetsu* 2, no. 7 (1929): 52–53.

3. "Ubume/Kosodate-Yūrei." Source: Kondō Kiichi, "Shintatsu Mintan-shū: Yūrei no hanashi, Komochi yūrei," in *Okinawa,*

vol. 1 of *Nihon Minzokushi Taikei*, edited by Ikeda Yaseburō et al. (Tokyo: Kadokawa-shoten, 1975), 96. See also Konno En-suke, *Nihon kaidan-shū: Yūrei-hen*, 292–312. Fanny Hagin Mayer, working from Yanagita's amassed volumes, mentions this legend on page 9 in *Ancient Tales in Modern Japan* (in a section entitled "Propitious Births"), and again in *The Yanagita Kunio Guide to the Japanese Folk Tale*, 9–10. In Japanese, see Yanagita Kunio, "Akagozuka no hanashi," in vol. 12 of *Teihon Yanagita Kunio-shū* (Tokyo: Chikuma-shobō, 1985), 214–51.

4. "Mosuke-Inari." Source: Tsukamoto Atsuo, "Kishū-Densetsu—Fukiagedera no Mosuke-Inari," *Tabi to Densetsu* 3, no. 4 (1930): 77. For a lengthy discussion and study of the fertility deities, see Nelly Naumann, "Yama-no Kami: The Japanese Mountain Deities," parts 1, 2, *Asian Folklore Studies* 22, no. 1 (1963): 133–366; 23, no. 2 (1964): 48–199.

5. "Obligations of a Dead Mother." Source: Kondō Kiichi, 96.

6. "A Nighttime Encounter." Source: Kondō Kiichi, 96. Dorson, in *Folk Legends of Japan* (Rutland and Tokyo: Tuttle, 1961), 97–99, unites into one item the three legends we have entitled "Obligations of a Dead Mother," "A Nighttime Encounter," and "Ubume/Kosodate-Yūrei." Rolf Wilhelm Brednich provides a modern German parallel ("Geburt im Grab") in *Die Spinne in der Yucca-Palme: Sagenhafte Geschichten von Heute* (Munich: C.H. Beck, 1990), 138–39; Brednich calls attention to its relation to the internationally known tale type, "Das unruhige Grab" (the restless grave), AaTh 760. For more information on *mizuko kuyō*, see Eiki Hoshino and Dosho Takeda, "Indebtedness and Comfort: The Undercurrents of *Mizuko Kuyō* in Contemporary Japan," *Japanese Journal of Religious Studies* 14 (December 1987): 305–20; and William R. La Fleur, *Liquid Life: Abortion and Buddhism in Japan* (Princeton: Princeton University Press, 1992). We are indebted to Kanako Shiokawa for calling this current arena of discussion to our attention.

7. "The Ghost of the Tofu Seller's First Wife." Source: Teraishi Masamichi, "Shōmeiji mae no yūrei" in *Chugoku-Shikoku*, vol. 3 of *Nihon Minzokushi Taikei*, edited by Ikeda Yasaburō et al. (Tokyo: Kadokawa-shoten, 1975), 226. The power of the written word, especially in sutra form, is illustrated by Lafcadio Hearn's novel *Miminashi-Hoichi*, taken from early Japanese tradition, in which a young monk is protected from samurai ghosts by sutras written all over his body. His abbot forgets to write on the monk's ear, however, and a frustrated samurai *yūrei* takes what he can, cutting off the ear with his sword.

8, 9. "A Little Girl's House Ghost"; "Two Child House Ghosts." Source: Sasaki Kizen, "Ōshū no Zashikiwarashi no hanashi," in *Tohoku*, vol. 9 of *Nihon Minzokushi Taikei*, edited by Ikeda Yasaburō et al. (Tokyo: Kadokawa-shoten, 1975), 172.

10. "The Fidelity of a Mother's Spirit." Source: Teraishi Masamichi, "Bōrei no Aichaku," in vol. 3 of *Nihon Minzokushi Taikei*, 224.

11, 12. "The Ghost of a Young Girl"; "Chūta's Ghost." Source: Kondō Kiichi, 96.

13. "Zentoku Bugs." Source: Yuasa Takaharu, "Zentokumushi no Meishō to Densetsu no Bunpu," *Tabi to Densetsu* 4, no. 6 (1931): 31. On the subject of *goryō*, see Hori, *Folk Religion in Japan*, 112–17, 199–200.

14, 15. "Nangakubō, the Mountain Hermit"; "The Blind Monk with the Bamboo Staff." Source: Hirata Yoshimitsu, "Rikuzen Asahiura ni Densetsu o tazunete," *Tabi to Densetsu* 4, no. 2 (1931): 72.

16. "The Alcoholic Monk." Source: Matsukawa Jirō, "Min'yō Densetsu o tazunete—Mikunibushi to Tōjinbō," *Tabi to Densetsu* 1, no. 3 (1928): 23–24.

17. "A Mountain Priest's Family Killed by Wolves." Source: Teraishi Masamichi, "Ōkami ni korosareshi Yamabushi-Oyako San'nin no Rei," in vol. 3 of *Nihon Minzokushi Taikei*, 227. Also see Hori, *Folk Religion of Japan*, 141–79, especially 156–60 and 170, note 58. A very good description of the *yamabushi* is given under "Bergasketen" by O. Rotermund in *Japan Handbuch*, edited by Horst Hammitzsch (Stuttgart: Franz Steiner Verlag, 1984), 1544–50.

18. "Hidarugami in the Mountains." Source: Kojima Chibuya, "Hidarugami no koto," *Tabi to Densetsu* 4, no. 8 (1931): 56.

19. "Hidarugami in Town." Source: Yamazaki Yoshikuni, "Yamaguchi-ken Ōshima-gun no Densetsu to Hōgen," *Tabi to Densetsu* 3, no. 5 (1930): 19.

20. "The Hunting Dog's Revenge." Source: Shigeno Yūkō, "Nansei-shotō no Densetsu—Aijin to utatta Katemen no Bōrei," *Tabi to Densetsu* 1, no. 8 (1928): 52.

21. "The Bell at Myōhō-san Temple." Source: Tsukamoto Atsuo, "Kishū-Densetsu—Myōhō-san no Hitotsugane," *Tabi to Densetsu* 3, no. 8 (1930): 50.

22. "Kechibi Foxfire in Hokkekyōdō." Source: Teraishi Masamichi, "Tosa-Fūzoku to Densetsu," in vol. 3 of *Nihon Minzokushi Taikei*, 205.

23. "The Two Wrestling Ghosts." Source: Naraki Noriyuki, "Kagoshima no Densetsu," *Tabi to Densetsu* 4, no. 3 (1931): 32.

24, 25. "A Bride Rescued from Her Fate"; "The Young Man and the Carving Knife." Source: Shigeno Yūkō, 52–53.

26, 27, 28, 29. "Mushrooms as Omens of Death"; "Audible Death Omens"; "The Aunt's Dream"; "A Drowning Omen." Source: Iwakiri Noboru, "Shi o Chūshin to shita Amami-Ōshima no Jitsuwa," *Tabi to Densetsu* 3, no. 9 (1930): 51–53.

30, 31, 32, 33, 34. "Ghosts in the Sea"; "Ghost Heads in the Water"; "The Ghost Ship"; "Ghost Ships and Ship Ghosts"; "The Shipwreck at Seto." Sources: Kodera Yūkichi, "Funa-Yūrei," *Tabi to Densetsu* 5, no. 6 (1932): 10; Sakurada Katsunori, "Funa-Yūrei," *Tabi to Densetsu* 5, no. 8 (1932): 22; Miyamoto Tsuneichi, "Suō-Ōshima—Iwa ni shigamitsuku," *Tabi to Densetsu* 3, no. 4 (1930): 52.

35. "The Ghost of the Temple Maiden." Source: Katō Ryūji, "Kyōdo Densetsu," *Tabi to Densetsu* 4, no. 3 (1931): 42.

36. A nicely translated version of "Botandōrō" by Donald Richie, based on several very early texts, is given in *Yanasen Magazine* 3 (n.d.): 2–4. It is followed by a brief account of Enchō the storyteller (5), and by a description of Yoshitoshi's (the famous printmaker of the 1800s) fascination with local Nezu-neighborhood ghosts in his works (by Jordan Sand, 6–8).

37, 38, 39. "The Spirit of a Loving Bondwoman"; "The Priest, His Niece, and the *Jitō*"; "Kiyo and Anchin." Sources: Shigeno Yūkō, 52–53. Nakamichi Hitoshi, "Eison-Hōin no Kai," *Tabi to Densetsu* 3, no. 1 (1930): 50–54. Sasaki Kizen, "Chō-Chū-Moku-Seki-Den," *Tabi to Densetsu* 3, no. 1 (1930): 65. Another version of the Anchin story is given in volume 2 of *We Japanese*, edited by Sakai Atsuharu, 68.

Suggested Reading

Much has been written about legend in recent years. For a basic working definition and a discussion of the relations and differences among *legend, folktale* and *myth*, Elliott Oring's essay, "Folk Narratives," in *Folk Groups and Folklore Genres*, edited by Elliott Oring (Logan: Utah State University Press, 1986), 121–45, is helpful and illuminating. Several books by Jan H. Brunvand have spotlighted the "urban legend" in contemporary U.S. tradition; of them, the first, *The Vanishing Hitchhiker: American Urban Legends and Their Meaning* (New York: Norton, 1981), is most useful; see also Brunvand's chapter on "Legends and Anecdotes" in his *The Study of American Folklore*, 3d rev. ed. (New York: Norton, 1986), 158–85; Alan Dundes's essay, "Folk Ideas as Units of World View," appeared in the *Journal of American Folklore* 84 (1971): 93–103.

Early collecting of Japanese legends is documented to some extent by the source notes on the legends in this book, but of course there are equivalent collections for virtually every locale and prefecture in Japan. Recent work on Japanese legends and legend theory has been produced by Konno Ensuke, *Nihon kaidan-shū: Yūrei-hen* (Tokyo: Shakaishisō-sha, 1969); Kondō Kiichi, "Shintatsu Mintan-shū: Yūrei no hanashi, Komochi yūrei," in *Okinawa*, vol. 1 of *Nihon Minzokushi Taikei*, edited by Ikeda Yasaburō et al. (Tokyo: Kadokawa-shoten, 1975), 96; Ikeda Yasaburō, *Nihon no yūrei* (Tokyo: Chūōkōron-sha, 1974); Nomura Jun'ichi, *Mukashi-banashi-Denshō no Kenkyū* (Tokyo: Dōhōsha-shuppan, 1984); and Takeda Tadashi, *Yukiguni no Kataribe* (Tokyo: Hōsē University Press, 1985). Others, including standard encyclopedias of Japanese folklore (especially legends and beliefs), are listed in the general bibliography.

Unfortunately, much of this fine and exciting work remains untranslated into English, and thus the impact these studies could make on American legend theory has been minimalized. A recent work in English is Hayao Kawai, *The Japanese Psyche: Major Motifs in the Fairy Tales of Japan*, translated by Hayao Kawai and Sachiko Reece (Dallas: Spring Publications, Inc., 1988). While most of the interpretations are guided by Jungian perspectives and the motif identification by European standards (Aarne-Thompson, e.g.), thus leaving relatively untreated the Japanese understanding of these issues with regard to Japanese texts, the stories and their discussion are nonetheless enlightening.

Most of Yanagita's writings are also untranslated, but luckily a few important works are available to us through the efforts of Fanny Hagin Mayer in *The Yanagita Guide to the Japanese Folk Tale* (Bloomington: Indiana University Press, 1986)—in which legends and tales are discussed together—and in the books of Ronald Morse and other Americans who have translated a few of Yanagita's pieces. Japanese readers will have no difficulty finding abundant studies of Yanagita, and will already know his works. Non-Japanese would do well to obtain the small, but enlightening, paperback edited by J. Victor Koschmann, Ōiwa Keibō, and Yamashita Shinji, *International Perspectives on Yanagita Kunio and Japanese Folklore Studies*, Cornell University East Asia Papers, no. 37 (Ithaca: Cornell University Press, 1985); in it are assessments of Yanagita's impact on Japanese folklore and discussions, pro and con, of his methods and approaches. Nearly every essay quotes Yanagita in enough detail that a Western reader otherwise cut off from access by language can form a fairly rich—if basic—concept of the man and his work.

A very brief interview with Yanagita appears on pp. 50–53 of Richard Dorson's *Studies in Japanese Folklore* (Bloomington: Indiana University Press, 1963). An excellent assessment of Yanagita's work is Ronald A. Morse's, *Yanagita Kunio and the Folklore Movement: The Search for Japan's National Character and Distinctiveness* (New York: Garland Publishing, 1990). Karatani Kōjin's comments on Yanagita appear in his *Imi to iu yamai* [The meaning of "sickness"], 5th ed. (Tokyo: Kōdansha, 1992), 246–58, 288–92, and in *Hyūmoa to shite no yuibutsuron* [Materialism as Humor], (Tokyo: Chikuma-shobō, 1993), 258–280. At this writing, the most recent study of Yanagita in English is Kawada Minoru, *The Origin of Ethnography in Japan: Yanagita Kunio and His Times*, trans. Toshiko Kishida-Ellis (London and New York: Kegan Paul International, 1993).

Interestingly enough, Yanagita's insistence on the validity of the subjective perspective presaged the modern work of such folklorists as David Hufford, who is investigating the many legends and custom clusters which emanate from (and help to interpret) personally perceived psychological experiences (like "the Hag dream" or the "near-death experience") which turn out to be widespread. See David J. Hufford, *The Terror That Comes in the Night: An Experience-Centered Study of Supernatural Assault Traditions* (Philadelphia: University of Pennsylvania Press, 1982).

Bibliography

Abe Masamichi. *Nippon no yūreitachi —
On'nen no Keifu.* Tokyo:
Nichibō-shuppan-sha, 1975.

Addiss, Stephen, ed. *Japanese Ghosts and
Demons: Art of the Supernatural.* New
York: George Braziller, 1985.

Antoni, Klaus. "Yasukuni und der 'Schlim-
me Tod' des Kriegers." *Bochumer
Jahrbuch zur Ostasienforschung* 10
(1987): 161–92.

Asakura Haruhiko, Inokuchi Shōji, Okano
Hirohiko, and Matsumae Takeshi,
eds. *Shinwa Densetsu Jiten.* Tokyo:
Tokyodo-shuppan, 1963.

Beardsley, Richard K., J.W. Hall, and
R.E. Ward. *Village Japan.* Chicago:
University of Chicago Press, 1959.

Benedict, Ruth. *The Chrysanthemum and
the Sword: Patterns of Japanese Culture.*
Boston: Houghton Mifflin, 1946.

Brednich, Rolf Wilhelm. *Die Spinne in der
Yucca-Palme: Sagenhafte Geschichten
von Heute.* Munich: C. H. Beck, 1990.

Brunvand, Jan Harold. "Legends and
Anecdotes." In *The Study of American
Folklore,* 158–85. 3d rev. ed. New
York: Norton, 1986.

———. *The Vanishing Hitchhiker: American
Urban Legends and Their Meaning.*
New York: Norton, 1981.

Campbell, Joseph. *The Masks of God.* 4 vols. New York: Viking, 1959–68.

Dorson, Richard M. *Folk Legends of Japan.* Rutland, Vt. and Tokyo: Tuttle, 1961.

———, ed. *Studies in Japanese Folklore.* Bloomington: Indiana University Press, 1963.

Dundes, Alan. "Folk Ideas as Units of World View," *Journal of American Folklore* 84 (1971): 93–103.

Eder, Matthias. "Totenseelen und Ahnengeister in Japan." *Anthropos* 51 (1956): 97–112.

Ema Tsutomu, *Nihon-yōkaihenge-shi* (The history of ghosts and monsters). 6th ed. Tokyo: Chūōkōron-sha, 1984.

Fukuda K. et al. "High Prevalence of Isolated Sleep Paralysis: *Kanashibari* Phenomenon in Japan." *Sleep* 10 (1987): 279–86.

———. "Preliminary Study on Kanashibari Phenomenon: A Polygraphic Approach." *Japan Journal of Physiology, Psychology, and Psychophysiology* 7 (1989): 83–89.

Fujisawa Tokihiko. "Funayūrei no Meiro." *Tabi to Densetsu* 1, no. 7 (1928): 18–19.

Hammitzsch, Horst, ed. *Japan Handbuch.* Stuttgart: Franz Steiner Verlag, 1984.

Hearn, Lafcadio. *In Ghostly Japan.* Boston: Little, Brown & Co., 1899.

———. *Miminashi-Hoichi no hanashi.* Tokyo: Hokuseido Press, 1965.

———. *A Passional Karma, The Dream of a Summer Day.* Tokyo: Shunyodo, 1931.

Hirata Yoshimitsu. "Rikuzen Asahiura ni Densetsu o tazunete." *Tabi to Densetsu* 4, no. 2 (1931): 27, 72–73.

Hori Ichirō. "The Appearance of Individual Self-Consciousness in Japanese Religion and Its Historical Transformations." In *The Japanese Mind: Essentials of Japanese Philosophy and Culture*, edited by Charles A. Moore, 201–27. Honolulu: University of Hawaii Press, 1967.

———. *Folk Religion in Japan: Continuity and Change.* Chicago: University of Chicago Press, 1968.

———. "Nihonjin no Reikon Kan'nen." In *Nihon-shūkyō no Shakaiteki Yakuwari*, 161–212. Tokyo: Miraisha, 1983.

Hoshino Eiki and Takeda Dosho, "Indebtedness and Comfort: The Undercurrents of *Mizuko Kuyō* in Contemporary Japan," *Japanese Journal of Religious Studies* 14 (1987): 305–20.

Hrdličková, V. "Japanese Professional Storytellers." In *Folklore Genres*, edited by Dan Ben-Amos, 171–90. Austin: University of Texas Press, 1976.

Hufford, David J. *The Terror That Comes in the Night: An Experience-Centered Study of Supernatural Assault Traditions.* Philadelphia: University of Pennsylvania Press, 1982.

Ikeda Yasaburō. *Nihon no yūrei.* Tokyo: Chūōkōron-sha, 1974.

Inokuchi Shōji. *Nihon no Zokushin.* Tokyo: Kōbundō, 1975.

Iwakiri Noboru. "Shi o Chūshin to shita Amami-Ōshima no Jitsuwa." *Tabi to Densetsu* 3, no. 9 (1930): 51–53.

Karatani Kōjin. *Hyūmoa to shite no yuibutsuron* (Materialism as Humor). Tokyo: Chikuma-shobō, 1993.

———. *Imi to iu yamai* (The meaning of "sickness"). 5th ed. Tokyo: Kōdansha, 1992.

Katō Ryūji. "Kyōdo Densetsu." *Tabi to Densetsu* 4, no. 3 (1931): 42.

Kawada Minoru. *The Origin of Ethnography in Japan: Yanagita Kunio and His Times.* Translated by Toshiko Kishida-Ellis. London and New York: Kegan Paul International, 1993.

Kawai Hayao. *The Japanese Psyche: Major Motifs in the Fairy Tales of Japan.* Translated by Hayao Kawai and Sachiko Reece. Dallas: Spring Publications, Inc., 1988.

Keije, Nikolas. *Japanese Grotesqueries.* Rutland, Vt. and Tokyo: Tuttle, 1973.

Kindaichi Kyōsuke et al. *Nihon Kokugo Daijiten.* 6th ed. Tokyo: Shōgakukan, 1986.

Kishimoto Hideo. "Some Japanese Cultural Traits and Religions." In *The Japanese Mind: Essentials of Japanese Philosophy and Culture,* edited by Charles A. Moore, 110–21. Honolulu: University of Hawaii Press, 1967.

Kodera Yūkichi. "Funa-Yūrei." *Tabi to Densetsu* 5, no. 6 (1932): 10.

Koike Nagayuki. *Hito no shigo no hanashi.* Tokyo: Gakugei Tosho, 1970.

Kojima Chibuya. "Hidarugami no koto." *Tabi to Densetsu* 4, no. 8 (1931): 56.

Kondō Kiichi. "Shintatsu Mintan-shū: Yūrei no hanashi, Komochi yūrei." In *Okinawa,* vol. 1 of *Nihon Minzokushi Taikei,* edited by Ikeda Yasaburō et al., 96. Tokyo: Kadokawa-shoten, 1975.

Konno Ensuke. *Barō kon'in-tan.* Tokyo: Iwasaki-Bijutsu-sha, 1956.

———. *Gendai no Meishin.* Tokyo: Shakaishisō-sha, 1961.

———. "Imikazu." In *Nihon Minzoku Jiten,* 55. Tokyo: Ōtsuka Minzoku Gakkai, Kōbundō-sha, 1980.

———. *Kaidan: Minzokugaku no Tachiba kara.* Tokyo: Shakaishisō-sha, 1957.

_____. _Nihon kaidan-shū: Yūrei-hen._ Tokyo: Shakaishisō-sha, 1969.

Koschmann, J. Victor, Ōiwa Keibō, and Yamashita Shinji, eds. _International Perspectives on Yanagita Kunio and Japanese Folklore Studies._ Cornell University East Asia Papers, no. 37. Ithaca: Cornell University Press, 1985.

La Fleur, William R. _Liquid Life: Abortion and Buddhism in Japan._ Princeton: Princeton University Press, 1992.

Maraini, Fosco. _Japan: Patterns of Continuity._ Tokyo and New York: Kōdansha International, 1971.

Matsudaira Narimitsu. "Tamashii." In _Studies in Japanese Folklore,_ edited by Richard M. Dorson, 181–97. Bloomington: Indiana University Press, 1963.

Matsukawa Jirō. "Min'yō Densetsu o tazunete—Mikunibushi to Tōjinbō." _Tabi to Densetsu_ 1, no. 3 (1928): 23–24.

Mayer, Fanny Hagin. _Ancient Tales in Modern Japan: An Anthology of Japanese Folk Tales._ Bloomington: Indiana University Press, 1984.

Meishin Chōsa Kyōgikai. _Nihon no Zokushin._ Rev. ed. 3 vols. Tokyo: Dōshisha, 1979.

Michener, James. _The Hokusai Sketch-Books: Selections from the Manga._ Tokyo and Rutland, Vt.: Tuttle, 1958.

Miyagi Otoya. _Shinpi no sekai—chōshinrigaku nyūmon_ (Introduction to parapsychology). Tokyo: Iwanami-shoten, 1961.

Miyamoto Tsuneichi. "Suō-Ōshima—Iwa ni shigamitsuku." _Tabi to Densetsu_ 3, no. 4 (1930): 52.

Miyata Noboru et al., eds. _Nihon Minzokugaku._ Tokyo: Kōbundō-sha, 1984.

Mizuki Shigeru, ed. _Mizuki Shigeru no yōkai-bunko_ (Mizuki Shigeru's paperback library of ghosts and monsters). 4 vols. Tokyo: Kawade-shobō-shinsha, 1984.

Mogami Takayoshi. "The Double Grave System." In _Studies in Japanese Folklore,_ edited by Richard M. Dorson, 167–80. Bloomington: Indiana University Press, 1963.

Mori Mashio. "Sai no Yonaki-ishi." _Tabi to Densetsu_ 2, no. 7 (1929): 52–53.

Morohashi Tetsuji et al., eds. _Shin-Kanwa-Jiten._ Tokyo: Taishūkan-sha, 1982.

Morse, Ronald A. _Yanagita Kunio and the Folklore Movement: The Search for Japan's National Character and Distinctiveness._ New York and London: Garland Publishing, 1990.

Nakamichi Hitoshi. "Eison-Hōin no Kai." _Tabi to Densetsu_ 3, no. 1 (1930): 50–54.

Nakamura Hajime, Fukagawa Koji, Tamura Yoshiro, and Imano Tatsushi, eds. *Iwanami bukkyo jiten* (Iwanami's Buddhist Dictionary). Tokyo: Iwanami shoten, 1989.

Naraki Noriyuki. "Kagoshima no Densetsu." *Tabi to Densetsu* 4, no. 3 (1931): 32.

Naumann, Nelly. "Yama-no kami: The Japanese Mountain Deities." Parts 1, 2. *Asian Folklore Studies* 22 (1963): 133–366; 23, no. 2 (1964): 48–199.

Nihon Daijiten Kankōkai. *Nihon Kokugo Daijiten.* Tokyo: Shōgakukan, 1986.

Nomura Jun'ichi. *Mukashi-banashi-Denshō no Kenkyū.* Tokyo: Dōhōsha-shuppan, 1984.

Nomura Jun'ichi et al., eds. *Nihon Densetsu Taikei.* Tokyo: Mizuumi-shobō, 1982– .

Ono Shūfū. "Shinda Hito no kuru Hanashi." *Tabi to Densetsu* 4, no. 6 (1931): 73.

Oring, Elliott. "Folk Narratives." In *Folk Groups and Folklore Genres*, edited by Elliott Oring, 121–45. Logan: Utah State University Press, 1986.

Ōshima Takehiko. *Hanashi no Denshō.* Tokyo: Iwasaki-Bijutsu-sha, 1984.

Ōtsuka-Minzoku-Gakkai. *Nihon Minzoku-jiten.* Tokyo: Kōbundō, 1971.

Plutschow, Herbert. "The Fear of Evil Spirits in Japanese Culture." *Transactions of Japan*, 3d s. 18 (1983): 133–51.

Radin, Paul. "Folktales of Japan as Told in California." *Journal of American Folklore* 59 (1946): 289–308.

Richie, Donald. "Botandōrō—The Peony Lantern," *Yanesen Magazine* 3 (n.d.), 2–4.

Sakai Atsuharu, ed. *We Japanese.* 3 vols. Miyanoshita, Japan: Fujiya Hotel, various dates.

Sakurada Katsunori. "Funa-Yūrei." *Tabi to Densetsu* 5, no. 8 (1932): 22.

Sasaki Kizen. "Chō-Chū-Moku-Seki-Den." *Tabi to Densetsu* 3, no. 1 (1930): 65.

———. "Ōshū no Zashikiwarashi no hanashi." In *Tohoku*, vol. 9 of *Nihon Minzokushi Taikei*, edited by Ikeda Yasaburō et al., 172. Tokyo: Kadokawa-shoten, 1975.

Seki Keigo. "Funa yūrei no hanashi 2-dai." *Tabi to Densetsu* 1, no. 4 (1928): 98–101.

Shigeno Yūkō. "Nansei-shotō no Densetsu—Aijin to utatta Katemen no Bōrei." *Tabi to Densetsu* 1, no. 8 (1928): 52–53.

Smith, Robert J. *Ancestor Worship in Contemporary Japan.* Palo Alto: Stanford University Press, 1974.

————. "The Life Cycle." In *Japanese Character and Culture*, edited by Bernard S. W. Silberman, 187–213. Tucson: University of Arizona Press, 1962.

Sunada Toshiko. *Japanese Food and Good Old Wisdom*. Tokyo: Ajinomoto Co., 1985.

Suwa Haruo, *Nihon no yūrei* (Japanese Ghosts). Tokyo: Iwanami-shoten, 1988.

Tada Michitarō. "Japanese Sensibility: An 'Imitation' of Yanagita." In *International Perspectives on Yanagita Kunio and Japanese Folklore Studies*, edited by J. Victor Koschmann, Ōiwa Keibō, and Yamashita Shinji, 97–120. Cornell University East Asia Papers, no. 37. Ithaca: Cornell University Press, 1985.

Takada Mamoru, *Edo-kaidan-shu* (A collection of ghost stories from Edo). 3d ed. 3 vols. Tokyo: Iwanami-shoten, 1989.

Takeda Tadashi. *Yukiguni no Kataribe*. Tokyo: Hōsē University Press, 1985.

Teraishi Masamichi. "Bōrei no Aichaku." In *Chugoku-Shikoku*, vol. 3 of *Nihon Minzokushi Taikei*, edited by Ikeda Yasaburō et al., 224. Tokyo: Kadokawa-shoten, 1975.

————. "Ōkami ni korosareshi Yamabushi-Oyako San'nin no Rei." In vol. 3. of *Nihon Minzokushi Taikei*, 227.

————. "Shōmeiji mae no yūrei," In vol. 3 of *Nihon Minzokushi Taikei*, 226.

————. "Tosa-Fūzoku to Densetsu." In vol. 3 of *Nihon Minzokushi Taikei*, 205.

Tsukamoto Atsuo. "Kishū-Densetsu—Fukiagedera no Mosuke-Inari." *Tabi to Densetsu* 3, no. 4 (1930): 75–77.

————. "Kishū-Densetsu—Myōhō-san no Hitotsugane." *Tabi to Densetsu* 3, no. 8 (1930): 50.

Ueda Makoto, ed. *The Mother of Dreams and Other Short Stories: Portrayals of Women in Modern Japanese Fiction*. Tokyo, New York, San Francisco: Kōdansha International, 1986.

Ueno Kazuo, Miyata Noboru, Fukuda Akira, and Takakuwa Morifumi, eds. *Shinpan Minzokuchōsa Handbook*. Tokyo: Yoshikawa-Kōbunkan-sha, 1987.

Umegaki Minoru. *Nihon no Imikazu*. Tokyo: Iwasaki-Bijutsu-sha, 1973.

Watanabe Shōkō. *Shigo no sekai*. Tokyo: Iwanami-shoten, 1959.

Yamaori Tetsuo. *Shi no minzokugaku: Nihonjin no shishōkan to sōsōgirei*. (The folklore of death: Japanese concepts of death and life and burial rituals). 2d ed. Tokyo: Iwanami-shoten, 1990.

Yamashita Shinji. "Ritual and 'Unconscious Tradition': A Note on *About Our Ancestors*." In *International Perspectives on Yanagita Kunio and Japanese Folklore Studies*, edited by J. Victor Koschmann, Ōiwa Keibō, and Yamashita Shinji, 55–64.

Yamazaki Yoshikuni. "Yamaguchi-ken Ōshima-gun no Densetsu to Hōgen." *Tabi to Densetsu* 3, no. 5 (1930): 19.

Yanagita Kunio. "Akagozuka no hanashi." In vol. 12 of *Teihon Yanagita Kunio-shū*, 214–51. Tokyo: Chikuma-shobō, 1985.

———. "Densetsu." In vol. 5 of *Teihon Yanagita Kunio-shū*, 1–328.

———. *Kinkishūzokugoi.* Tokyo: Kokugakuin Daigaku Hōgen Kenkyūkai, 1938.

———. *The Legends of Tōno.* 1910. New ed. Tokyo: The Japan Foundation Translation Series, 1975.

———. *Nihon Densetsu Meii.* Tokyo: Nihon Hōsō Kyōkai, 1950.

———. "Senzo no hanashi." In vol. 10 of *Teihon Yanagita Kunio-shū*, 1–152.

———. *Sōsō shūzoku goi.* Tokyo: Iwanami-shoten, 1937.

———. *The Yanagita Kunio Guide to the Japanese Folk Tale.* Translated and edited by Fanny Hagin Mayer. Bloomington: Indiana University Press, 1986.

Yuasa Takaharu. "Zentokumushi no Meishō to Densetsu no Bunpu." *Tabi to Densetsu* 4, no. 6 (1931): 31.

Index